JOURNEY *of a* SOUL

To Our Readers,

We are dedicated to publishing books that enrich the spirit and to bring to the universe messages for each spirit to develop greater connection to the Eternal Life Source. *The Journey to Spiritual Awareness* series is three books written for this purpose. *Journey of A Soul, An Exploration of Spirit* is the first. It will be followed by, *Heart of A Soul, An Exploration of Abundance,* and *Truth of A Soul, An Exploration of Universal Divinity.*

With blessings of joy and peace to you on your journey,

JAMAR PUBLISHERS

JOURNEY *of a* SOUL

An Exploration of Spirit

Margaret Feathers

JaMar Publishing

Published by JaMar Publishing, 2001
E-mail: jamarpublishing@aol.com

ISBN: 0-9709116-0-2

Library of Congress Control Number 2001126251

Printed in the United States of America

I dedicate this book to
my children, David and Lynne,
and my daughter-in-law, Danya.
They fill my life with joy.

Contents

Prologue

She told me just to type, she would help me. "She" is called Goswain and she is one of my guides. I have several and they come to help me during this lifetime. I have journeyed here before and I may be here again. Each journey is to learn and grow into a higher spirit—the spirit I am meant to be—always the same and yet always growing, evolving as we are all meant to do.

The words are not hers; she is but a messenger for the Highest Spirit, the Giver of Life, the Essence of

All—the Voice of God. Does this seem strange to you? I will admit at one time it did to me also, but now I know that we all have His voice inside us, all the time. We have but to still ourselves and we will hear it. Goswain has come to help me bring this knowledge to you by way of this book. Her purpose is to help me put my knowing on these pages.

I remember the first time I received the message from the Spirit that I was to write a book. I was amazed. My first reaction was, "What?!? You want me to write a book? How in the world will I do that? I don't even know what it is to be about!" But I was told not to worry. Then I received another message some time later while I was meditating. It was very powerful. The Highest Voice came to me, bathing me in love, telling me, "Love me. Trust me. Believe me. Follow where I lead and you will know." He repeated the entire message and added, "Write your book." The entire time I was in His presence tears were rolling down my cheeks. It was a gentle presence, very quiet and soothing. It was beautiful, overwhelming and wondrous and I was wrapped in love and peace.

I felt so gifted and blessed and truly loved, a love which no words in any language can explain. I knew I was not to worry, not think about the process of writing. It was all taken care of. All I had to do was trust. I still didn't know the format of the book, but I knew I was to share my story and I knew it was to be.

So, I begin. Another step on my journey, to share what I have experienced and hopefully, to impart to you the wonder I have known—the Wonder of All. And to show you the total communion you can have with the Highest of Spirits if you reach out, open your heart and soul and allow Him in and allow the abundance of His universe to flow through you. A treasury of gifts awaits you, to your heart, your soul and your physical being—our complete spirits.

I invite you to travel with me.

CHAPTER 1

The Cry

Once there was a soul who cried out in pain—and it was I. That pain and that cry began my journey, heartfelt, peaceful and painful, and leading to a blessed, joyful end. Not an ending as in time, but an ending as in a need to seek no further. Yes, an ending, but also a beginning—that of a joyful exploration of the spirit, His and mine. An exploration of the abundance of His universe, one He is privileged to shower upon each and every one of us as His children. We are all blessed in His name. We are all—or can be—one with Him if we reach for Him and commit ourselves to His presence. I call Him God, the Supreme and High Spirit of all that is, of all creation, of the entire universe.

How does my story begin? What brought me to the point in my life where I was in such pain? How did I get there and now, here? What was my process? What were my questions and, more importantly, what were my answers? Who was sent to help me? Who is with me still? What were my challenges, struggles and heartaches in the search for my answers? How did I learn to listen? How do I listen now? How did I learn to trust, to search, to experience the pain and exhilaration of discovery? Most wondrous of all, how did I come to *KNOW*? How did I learn about knowing, the knowing that comes from a place in the depths of the soul? How did I learn of that which gives such a sense of peace and presence of the Spirit that nothing in the world can diminish it; the knowing that brings with it a oneness, a unity so strong, so invincible, so complete that it is untouchable by anything other than His presence?

These, and more, are the questions we will explore. The answers will free your heart and soul, your total spirit if you trust in His words on these pages. My story I give to you so you too can experience the oneness I know; the joy that has filled my life; the abundance that is showered upon me; the gladness and rejoicing that is in my heart. And the inexplicable, complete and total love that is mine every moment in the universe, His universe that He has blessed me with. My heart is full and overflowing with the abundance of His love.

My story begins years ago as one in a large family of twelve children. I, being the fourth oldest, often cared for my younger brothers and sisters. It was a family much blessed by love and security, but also with hardship and difficulty. My father and mother worked very hard in taking care of us and we never lacked for the essentials. We did not have what one would consider the "luxuries" of life, but we always had good food on the table and clean clothes to wear. My parents tried hard to give us special times, but with so many children, it was difficult to always meet the individual needs of each one of us. I bless and thank them for what they, from the goodness of their hearts, gave to each of us. But there were times we reached for each other, as brothers and sisters, for our support, our comfort and our love. We learned to fight, but also to love. We learned anger, but also forgiveness. We learned jealousy, but also gladness in each other.

We learned fear and confusion, but also peace and simplicity. Why do I tell you this? Because it will help you to understand that I am from a family just like any other. I am no different from you or your family, or anyone else you may know. I am who I am. Just as you are who you are. I have found my way to this oneness with the Most High Spirit and so too, can you.

My married life also taught me much. It too, taught me love, but again, also anger and fighting, fear and confusion. This lasted much too long before I listened to my heart and not my head and filed for divorce. For you see, the anger and fighting, fear and confusion reached a point where it overcame the love, the kind of love a husband and wife must have to be one union. One cannot learn to live without that love. Before you believe that we, my former husband and I, did not love each other in the beginning, I must tell you that we did. That love was not nourished however, as it could have been, so it was best to part. We do carry each other in a special place in our hearts to this day.

It is not yet necessary for you know more of the details of my life or marriage. Know only that I was at a crossroads. I felt tremendous pain from the weight of my life and knew that I could not continue as I was. I was responsible for so many others, but I was neglecting myself. The pain and heartache was more than I could bear any longer. A choice had to be made—continue as I was, trying the best I could, but being unhappy and sad, or alter my life. I came to know what to do over time as I searched for an answer.

One night as I lay in bed trying to sleep, I had reached a point of such despair and sadness, that I knew I could not go on with my life as it was for another day. Feeling burdened and tearful, I did the only thing left for me to do. I reached for God and said, "You have to help me. I cannot do this one more day." It was the cry from my heart. Immediately, an all-consuming heat came over me. It began in my feet and slowly traveled up my body until it culminated in my head with an intensity and a power so strong I thought I would explode from the force of it. It was tremendous and I felt on fire. Then, just as slowly, it traversed down my body, cooling and leaving in its place a calm and a peace such as I had never to that point experienced in my life. The peace entered and surrounded me. It bathed me in its presence and I immediately fell asleep.

I awoke the next morning feeling refreshed, for the first time in months, and remembered what had happened. The peace was still with me and the burdens of my life did not seem quite so painful, so overwhelming or so despairing. I knew the Spirit had touched me. I knew He had heard my cry for help and answered it with His love and His peace. This was the first of many times since that He has made His presence known to me. That night of immense pain and the cry from my soul began my spiritual journey in force, in oneness with Him.

Lest you believe I did not call on Him before at times in my life, this is not true. But even in asking for His help, I did not hear His voice. I did not hear His messages for me. I did not listen. I tried to do all by myself. I traveled my life as I thought I was to do. The voices I heard were not His, they were often not even my own. Mine—the voice of my heart—was lost in the voices of those around me and lost in the voice of my head. Those voices talked of "should" and "must" and "have to". They spoke of demand and anger and responsibility. They were of others defining my role, my life and my boundaries. In essence, trying to define who I was. Finally though, the voice of my heart broke free and with that cry for help and the beautiful, loving voice that answered, I was set free. I was free as never before.

My life has not been the same since and I am eternally grateful. The joy that now envelops my life I am unable to explain. Happiness and peace surround me. I am free to be. I am one with the Spirit. He is in me as I am in Him. We are one, as we all can be with Him. He wishes for us to be. He awaits our cry, our asking, and our union with Him. For He is *with* us at all times, but He wishes to be *in* us at all times. So it is with us now—He and I. We are one.

Follow me as I tell you of Him.

CHAPTER 2

The Beginning

Where do we begin in this exploration of God? For this is our purpose here in these pages—to explore the Creator. Well, the only way is to go to the Source. How is this done? Very simply, really, we just ask. That's all there is to it, we just ask. He is waiting for the moment when we reach for Him. He is eagerly awaiting our voice. For one thing we must understand is, He is nothing without us. Now, when I was first told this, I was astounded. God!! Nothing without us?!? Nothing without me?!? This was too much for me to comprehend. It certainly wasn't what I had been previously taught. It certainly is not what churches teach. It goes against the principles of organized religion. But through the process of my spiritual growth, my spiritual pathway, I have come to understand how we are united, how we are one. As He is, I am. Are you shocked? We are exactly the same? How can I say this? What can I mean? I can say this for He says it and I know for He has told me.

Am I telling you He came as a voice in the night? Am I telling you He came as a quiet voice in my heart? Am I telling you He came as a gentle presence surrounding me in the light of His love? Am I telling you our souls are connected, that there is no separation between us? Am I telling you this and more? My answer is "Yes" to all of these questions.

You may doubt these statements. I understand, for I too, did not know these things. Now, however, my journey has led me to this knowing of Him. I have been directed and guided and led and protected and loved the whole way to union with Him. You might ask why this is so. Again, the answer is very simple—I asked for Him to enter my life. That's all I did. I opened my heart and simply asked. He is a being so profound, so wondrous, so caring and loving we cannot imagine the depths of His love for us. But we can feel it. Each time He is in my presence in a way that I can physically and soulfully feel Him, I am overcome with emotion. I am frequently moved to tears. I well with a sense of caring and loving that words cannot describe.

How did I reach this point, of this knowing Him? Was it an easy journey? Was it a challenge? Was it painful? Was it joyful? Was it beautiful? It was all of these. There were times I would throw my hands up and say, "What do you want now? I don't know what you are asking me or telling me, and frankly, right now, you must leave me alone!" There were times I begged for His messages when He had been quiet too long. There were times I was frustrated, then elated; happy, then sad; angry, then forgiving. For my faith and trust were certainly challenged. But it was all for purpose. It was all as is was to be. It was all to bring me to Him in the way that lights my life with a joy that radiates from me.

Am I so different from you? Am I unlike others that I have this and they do not? I know I am not. I know with every fiber of my being and every particle of my heart and soul that everyone can experience my joy, my happiness, my faith and trust. I am no different from you. The most beautiful thing is that He wants joy and happiness and completeness for every single one of His children. We are all His creation and to His creation, He will give all in His universe.

You need to know of my experience. You need to know of my journey to the peace that surrounds me. You need to know of how His love has changed my life. You need to know how knowing Him has given my life its purpose—to tell my story so that you too may be led to Him.

Follow me.

CHAPTER 3

Learning

My life has been one of giving and taking care of others. As I have said previously, I was lost in this giving. Yes, I gave of a generous spirit for this was what I felt, but it was also one of duty and obligation. Most, but not all, was through a loving heart, but I came to the point in which I felt I was drowning from the weight of my responsibility.

As one of a large family and as one of the eldest daughters, I was required to help care for my younger brothers and sisters. I learned to care for babies and cook and clean at an early age. Did I resent this or was I mean-spirited because of it? I can honestly answer "No" because it was just a fact of my life. It did prepare me for my married life and in caring for and raising my children and for this I am grateful. But is it a way I would prefer to repeat? I can again answer "No" because it, to a large extent, did not allow me to be a child, to be cared for as I needed to be cared for or to experience the childlike innocence of youth. Through my school years, I did have fun, but always with the obligation of responsibility demanding attention first. It was the way of my life and I accepted it.

I married two years after my high school graduation. Four years after my wedding, I gave birth to my precious son and almost two years after that, to my beautiful daughter. I worked as a secretary for a major automobile company in Detroit until my son's birth. It was important to me to raise my children and I was fortunate to be able to remain home with them until they were both in school full-time. I then returned to the workforce, but now as a dental assistant for a local dentist. I worked there for several years until I decided to pursue earning an undergraduate degree. Working part-time and going to school part-time, five years after my admission into college, I graduated with a Bachelor's Degree in Occupational Therapy and began working in the rehabilitation department for a major community hospital. I enjoyed my work and loved the interaction with my peers and caring for my patients. It was a blessed time in my life and I will always treasure the opportunities for growth I had both personally and professionally.

The details of my life may be different from yours but basically, are probably much the same, too. You can see I am no different from anyone else, no different from you. I hope also you can see since it was possible for me to find this glorious soul peace and happiness, so too, can you.

The real purpose of my life however, was and is my journey into my spirituality, my soul journey that began in earnest with my cry for help. My journey has led me to many new experiences in my search for self, truth and peace. Through my journey, in my search for my essence and in my exploration of Him, I learned much.

- I learned to quiet my mind and my body.
- I learned to find the core of me and still it.
- I learned to listen to the voice within and the voices of guides and angels sent to help me.

- I learned to ask questions and seek answers.
- I learned of healing and its great power.
- I learned to heal and to help others in a different way, the way of true connection, the connection of love.
- I learned that love could be transferred through time and space to heal.
- I learned we are pure energy—energy which is one with all other energy in the universe and all connected.
- I learned to feel what I was feeling, honestly and without reservation or restriction.
- I learned to cry and feel true pain, the pain of release and cleansing.
- I learned to laugh out loud.
- I learned of forgiveness.
- I learned the love of self.
- I learned of His love and therefore, all love.
- I learned to trust, to believe, to know of His presence.
- I learned I am nothing without Him. Period. Nothing.
- And, I learned to rejoice.

Come, so you may learn also.

CHAPTER 4

Presence

Meditation was a powerful experience for me in my connection with the Spirit and His other emissaries. Finding the core of self—the essence of who you are—releases you from all physical and concrete ties to this universe. It frees you to experience and understand a higher you, you that is trapped in the demands of the day, the weight of responsibility and the thousand voices and abundant noise you hear all day long. It is what gives you, you. This is where He resides, in partnership with you, in union with you, and in Oneness with you.

I began mediation listening to the Gregorian Chants. I played a tape of this music using headphones and it helped me in the beginning to concentrate on a certain sound to lessen the outside noise. It helped me to focus. I continued this way until the music itself became a distraction and I stopped using it. I could by then quiet myself very easily and free my spirit and hear my inner voice.

I must tell you that I experienced several things during meditation. I felt the presence of "others" and I will never forget the first and only time I heard an actual audible voice speaking to me when no one else was in the house. This occurred when I was still using the headphones. The voice was external, very loud and spoke very fast. It was a male voice and completely unintelligible. It reminded me of someone in charge of a news program, organizing several things at the same time and barking orders to everyone, the one in charge who had everything under control. This is the voice I heard. At first, I thought it was coming from the headset I was wearing, that somehow I had switched from the tape to the radio. Then I realized there was no radio on the tape player. It startled and frightened me at first. It certainly got my attention and I believe this was completely what it was meant to do—get my attention in a big way! I came to realize though that it was a way to let me know I was to listen and continue what I was doing—seeking and learning. There were messages for me. There was purpose in what I was doing and what I was to do. I was to continue to seek and learn. The voice never returned but rather, was replaced over time with many other quieter and softer voices that spoke much clearer messages.

I spoke earlier of the "others" whose presence I felt. I hope I can explain this in a way you can "feel" what I mean. Along our journey in this lifetime on this earth plane, we are never alone. Yes, we travel with the Spirit if this is our choice, but we also travel with those sent by Him to help and guide us. To believe we humans are the highest evolved beings of His creation is very limiting and does not speak of His greatness. For if we consider all levels of the Spirit, and compare them to the ones we impose on ourselves as human beings, we must conclude there are higher and greater entities than those we consciously know. These are the ones who travel with us, our angels and guides. These are the ones He has sent in His generosity and love to bring us to Him. For this is all He desires—for us to be one with Him in love.

My first "other" was not an angel, or what is considered an angel. It was and is, a male figure, dressed as a monk in a brown garb. He is a joyous spirit and he "told" me his name, which is Enoch. Now, you ask, how did he tell me? Imagine you are in a room and you "sense" eyes staring at you. I believe you have felt this sensation before. You know you are being watched; you can feel the presence of another. When you search the room, you can find those eyes watching. You know you have found that presence. So too, it is when you "sense" your "others". You are aware. You know. It is a gentle presence that comes to you quietly and completely and in peace. This is the way they "talk". It is a quiet and peaceful voice that enters your consciousness. It is a direct communication without an outside source such as we are accustomed to. Sounds strange, doesn't it? You may be thinking so, but it is really rather natural. Why believe communication is only that which can be seen, heard or measured? Again, this is limiting the power of the Creator. He is greater than this.

Enoch was the first of many guides who have come to me and he is with me still. He has told me in his gentle and complete way that he has been with me from my birth on this earth and will be with me until I am no longer physically here. He is now a part of me just as my arms and legs are and I would be lost without him. He travels in partnership with other guides at times and sometimes alone, and I take great comfort in knowing he is with me. (Thank you, Enoch, for your presence and guidance.) As I said, he will always be with me.

I also have several angels who travel with me who have made their presence known. All my guides and angels have given me their names and I have seen what they look like just as I did with Enoch. They are of all shapes and sizes, garbed as different as night and day. All have told me why they are with me, what their purpose is in helping me, and what it is they are to do to assist me on my journey. Some come and stay with me for only a short while until their work is done and then move on. Some stay for longer and longer periods of time helping me as needed to fulfill my purpose.

We all have purpose in this life. We all have a mission or goal that only we can achieve. Think of this. No one—absolutely no one else—can achieve what we are to do. Our sole, or rather, "soul" purpose is to learn to love, but we each have a particular way in which this is to be done. Through His love for us, He has blessed us with everything we need in order to do this, including the abundance of "others", our beautiful and generous guides and angels whose total purpose is to help us along our path. They are the epitome of unconditional love and support and ones who bless our lives.

During meditation, we connect with them because we are free of our conscious control of our psyche or mind or thoughts or whatever name we might give it. Know only that we can free ourselves to a different level, a higher level, a level that opens us to greater and greater heights of awareness and allows our spirit to run free. Am I saying we can experience an "out-of-body" awareness? Am I saying we can still be aware on a certain level of our physical being, but be totally separated from it at the same time? Am I saying we can be "in two places at the same time"? The answer is "Yes" to all these questions. Can this be done? How is it possible? Simply, we are so much more than we know. We are truly and completely and wonderfully His creation. If we believe we are His creation and we are created as He is, then how could it be that these things could not be possible, that they could not be real? They are. Do not limit the power of your creation.

Opening ourselves to a higher awareness brings with it an abundance of blessings. We are given sight of wonderful, glorious and beautiful visions of a universe far beyond our limited human knowledge. We are given sounds such as those unknown to the human ear. We are given peace and joy that is so abundant as to be uncontainable. We are given laughter and happiness and radiance which flows from us. And the most precious and glorious gift of all—we are given a love that is so deep, so profound, so complete, so unconditional and so total that it fills the essence of who we are. This love is the Creator. This love is who He is. This love is the Essence. I told you in the beginning we would explore who God is.

This is who He is—Total Love. Embracing. Endless. Complete.

CHAPTER 5

Forgiveness

Meditation was one way that brought me closer to the Spirit and an awareness of who He is. Another very powerful way was to learn forgiveness.

I had carried with me for a very long time anger that was robbing me of my freedom to be me. Anger can cripple and kill all other real emotion and feeling. It is a great way to deny feeling, deny joy, deny compassion, deny happiness, and deny truth from entering our lives. It is the greatest killer of all time. It stems from fear, which is the opposite of love. All emotion is either love or fear. If one is not bathed in love, it is because fear has taken over and pushed love aside. Love is the great healer. It frees our souls and spirits and gives life to all.

Why do we hang on so to our fear and then our anger? Why do we give it so much life? Why do we give it so much power? Why do we allow it to cripple us? I'm not sure I can answer these questions. I lived it myself and I don't know why it is so. Maybe it is because of insecurity, or denial, or want of control, or inability to let others into our lives because we are afraid of being hurt or scorned. Maybe it is simply we don't know how to listen to our hearts. Maybe we are so accustomed to pushing down the voice of our spirit and our soul that we reach a point where we can't hear it any longer and the voice of fear takes over. I don't know why, but I do know it does maim us and can destroy us if we let it.

I said earlier that most of my giving was of a pure heart, but not all of it. I did feel the weight of responsibility and obligation of caring for others in my personal life and I became angry because of it. I will share here some very personal history so you may understand.

My married life was often happy and blissful, but things changed. It was weighed down with the diagnosis of a severe medical condition that my former husband experienced. The details of this part of the story are his to share if he desires. Suffice it to say, for years he lived in a state of denial and did not take full responsibility for his condition. It did however, have a very serious effect on our family and it was left to me to hold the pieces together. I was responsible for monitoring his condition and medications, raising and taking care of our children, managing the household, going to work and school and helping with everyone's adjustment. After years of this, I did give into my resentment and anger and it began to destroy my giving heart. I was no longer able to give to him willingly and with love, nor he to me.

As his condition progressed, so, too, did the stress. It was difficult for all of us and our anger grew. It reached a point with me to where my heart nearly broke from the pain of it, and as I said before, I knew I could not go on one more day from it or the responsibility of my life. I was trapped by the weight of my emotions. I had, by not listening to myself, allowed despair and anger to wrap itself around my heart. This was when I cried for help. This was when I searched through the darkness for comfort, for relief from my pain and this was when He answered. He answered with peace, with hope, and with love. He answered with His voice. He was the one who was able to push the voice of fear and anger from my heart and allow His voice to enter. His was the voice that spoke to me of forgiveness.

I knew I needed to release and cleanse from my heart and soul, indeed, my total spirit, all the negativity I had allowed to enter. I needed to replace it with forgiveness and love and compassion. I asked for His help and, through the voice of a friend, He answered.

She was teaching a class I was attending and she spoke one night of forgiveness. She spoke of the need to rid ourselves of anger and pain in order to allow love, peace and joy to enter. An exercise was given to us that we could follow to help us to release and free our hearts. She instructed us to write a letter to those we were angry with. We were to experience all the feelings and emotions that were generated from this letter writing, to hold nothing back and to write as much and as powerful a letter as we needed. The only true requirement was to *feel*—to the core of us. Feel the pain, the anger, the resentment, the hostility, the hurt, the frustration, whatever it was we carried in our heart. Just feel.

We were then to burn the letter in such a way nothing would remain of it. All ashes would be given to the universe along with all our negative feelings. In the burning, we were to say, "Dear (name of person), I now release your energy back to you. I no longer need to carry it." Then we were to visualize a pure white light coming in filling the space of our heart, now free from all negativity and, at the same time, say, "Please fill this void with loving light toward myself."

One cannot understand the power of this exercise until he or she fully completes it. I will never forget my experience in this. I was alone one night in my house, totally free from all distractions and able to give myself completely to writing my letters. I wrote individual letters to a few different people and had worked up quite a state of true emotion. I then went into my kitchen to burn them in an old container I had. Each one was burned individually and the prayer said each time.

As the last one, which held the most anger, finished burning, I felt a power come over me with such a force that it pushed me back into a chair that was close by. I was overcome with emotion and tears were rolling down my cheeks. I was definitely surrounded with a presence so powerful and complete that I can still feel it to this day. It totally enveloped me, encasing me in its protection, holding me close and filling me with its light. It was so strong and so complete I was unable to stop crying or feeling its presence for a very long time. Then, the most beautiful thing happened. I was left with such a sense of peace that it radiated throughout my whole being. It consumed me. It transcended me to a place I had never been. It was a place of all perfect love—total perfection. I knew the Spirit had, once again, touched me. I knew it was His light I had been given. I knew it was His energy that was the force behind what I experienced. I knew my heart was filled with Him and all that He is.

For this too, is who He is. Forgiveness. Comfort. Peace. Power.

CHAPTER 6

Energy

My life has been enriched beyond measure since completing the forgiveness exercise. It has released anger from my life and allows my spirit peace. You may doubt my statement that I feel no anger in my life. I tell you, and whether you choose to believe it is your option, but it is so. I am able to allow others to be who they are and not be affected in a negative way from the energy that surrounds them. I can observe their behavior, words and actions, but not absorb them into my energy field.

What do I speak of now? What is this energy I mentioned?

Energy is a life force and we are totally and completely energy. All of life, in whatever form it takes, is energy. Everything in nature is energy. Everything in the universe is energy. So then, we are life forces. Not only are we in a physical sense, but also on other levels. Our thoughts, words, emotions, feelings, actions, words, behaviors—all are energy. We, as life forms, give energy. We also receive energy. What we give, we attract. An energy field that is one of the most powerful forces in the universe surrounds us.

The fact that we cannot see it with the naked eye does not mean it does not exist. It has been photographed and measured. It is very real. The problem is, we do not protect it. We allow it to be poked and jabbed and hurt until it can no longer fight to protect us. This is what fear and all that stems from it does. It destroys. Our energy is depleted. We are tired and drawn, unhappy and longing for peace. We allow all garbage surrounding the negativity of others or our society to enter us and destroy. We allow the destruction of ourselves. When I realized this, I was amazed.

I had allowed, as I said previously, for my life to reach that painful point. I had allowed others' demands and expectations of who I was to destroy my essence. My energy field came complete with gaping holes caused by lack of protection. Forgiveness began to close those holes. Forgiveness began my process of self-protection. Now I understand, *I* must protect my essence. *I* am responsible to do this, no one else. I now know in allowing anger to enter my life, *I* destroy myself. It can only destroy. Do you know of one great outcome that stemmed from anger? I do not. I have seen, as we all have, destruction of men and nations, children and societies, the environment and nature because of anger.

What in the world are we thinking? Why do we insist on continuing along this way? Why do we allow ourselves to destroy? Each one of us, one by one, must realize our part in this destruction. Each time an essence dies, or is even wounded, all of us are affected. Since we are all connected, our energy is not ours alone. Energy flows into other energy. There is no separation from one to another.

Picture two bodies of water that have come together and now flow as one. Can you tell where one stops and the other begins? It is not possible to do so. This is how it is with energy; it all flows as one. Understanding this, we must then understand how we—

each and every life form in the universe—are connected. This connection cannot be broken. If I am angry, that anger spills out to all who come in my path. If not protected, they absorb it and in turn pass it to everyone who comes in their path, and on and on it goes. The great destroyer is at work. Now imagine, if it works this way with negativity, it can work the same way with all that is positive. Love, peace, joy, happiness, contentment, acceptance, brotherhood, and healing can be passed from one to another. These—and all that is good—can be spilled into the next energy field and be passed on and on and on. These will soon surround all and will generate a most powerful source of oneness with all of life. The gaping holes of pain will be healed. The Source gives all this to us.

For He is this. Energy. Unity. Oneness. Healing.

CHAPTER 7

Healing

Healing. What a beautiful word. Let it settle into your consciousness for a moment. Let it surround you. Can you feel its comfort? Can you feel its beauty? Can you feel its power? I long for you to feel these, for healing is a most joyous and beautiful gift He has blessed us with.

I have a medical background and you can see much of my work, my occupation, has been in the health professions. I have a great respect for the medical technologies, interventions and treatments we use each and every day. But I now know of the real, true and most powerful way to heal. It is from self-giving and giving to others through love. What is this about?

All healing comes from the Highest Spirit. It is one of His most precious gifts to us and one that He is honored to give us. It is a treasure that we can employ to heal ourselves, others, the world, in fact, all in the universe. Healing travels beyond all earthly rhyme or reason or that which can be scientifically proven. I know there are skeptics to these statements and this is okay. It is not necessary for me to prove it in this dialogue; it is only for me to tell you what I know.

My first experience in healing was through a method called Reiki. It is a way of calling from the higher self to the highest being; to unite as one force to generate healing energy to aid in the completeness of an individual person, animal or plant, whatever life form healing is asked for. It is a way of asking and uniting for healing for the highest good of that being. It is a community of spirits coming together for the good of one and, of that one, then for all.

Reiki is a method. It is an intervention. It is a technique. All it asks for is healing from the Highest Power, through love, of love, by love and from love. There are many other methods, interventions and techniques that are called by different names—Healing Touch, prayer, and many more—which ask and do the same thing. What it is called does not matter. The methodology or ceremony does not matter. The techniques used do not matter. All that matters is love be a part of it. Remember I said all healing comes from the Highest Spirit? This is because healing incorporates love and love is the Highest Spirit. Love is God. There is no love without Him; therefore, there is no healing without Him. Sounds rather simple, doesn't it? Well, it is and it isn't.

The fact that all healing is from His eternal source is the easy part. The part that takes some work to understand is how it is done.

Healing takes love. Healing also takes connectedness, but connectedness to what or to whom? Remember when we spoke of energy and how all energy in the universe was connected, was one? If this is so, and it is, healing can be achieved through this oneness. This oneness is connected to the life force, God, as all life is connected to Him. God is power. God is all there is or needs to be. So, in connecting to the power that He is, we are able to "communicate" or transcend ourselves, and work through Him and His love in order to reach others to heal. Again, all that is needed is our intention to act through love in order to bring about the completeness of a life being. It is this intention that acts as a bridge uniting all healing energy. It is "moving across" this bridge that healing occurs. True healers know they are but an instrument of His divine healing love. They know they are the "bridge". They know they are uniting with other healers to bring about the higher good of a life being. Is it possible for one healer to act alone in healing? No, it is not. It is impossible, for remember, all energy is connected; energy is life and all life is connected to its Creator. To say a healer acts alone is to say his or her Creator does not exist.

We must also understand the power of a community of healers coming together for purpose. If one being is connected to the power of the Most High and that power has the ability to transcend time and space to heal, think of the power which is generated by a group or legion of healers. We all know the strength of a team of horses pulling a wagon in comparison to a lone horse pulling it. So it is with healing. A combined force connected to one another and all connected to the Supreme Being is a force that has a power that cannot be defined.

This is the power of healing through any methodology utilized. As I said earlier, it does not matter what the intervention is. The force of the power of intention to heal through love is all that is needed. Love is the Creator. Life is of the Creator. Energy is life. Healing is through energy and love. Therefore, healing is possible only with the Creator.

Giving to others for the purpose of healing is done in this manner of connection through love with the Creator. How does self-giving for the purpose of healing occur? It does in much the same way. Just as we said earlier, one cannot heal alone because all is connected to God. It stands to reason then, this same connectedness to the Spirit is how self-healing occurs. It is in this oneness that healing can and does occur.

We each have power that comes from our oneness with God. It is in this power that we create our own bridge to cross over to Him. We can place ourselves on this bridge any time we desire. We can seek union for this purpose whenever we wish. It is totally at our discretion to create our union with Him for this purpose. In union with Him, we are given the abundance of the universe and abundance includes healing for our higher good. He desires our higher good and will do all, from His love, for us to attain it. It is another of His gifts to us—our ability to heal ourselves.

Now, having said all this, you may be wondering about all of those happenings in our life that have dramatic effects on us that we seemingly cannot change. What is healing in relation to them?

These issues will be discussed in the following pages. For now, I wish for you to take a few moments to *feel* what you have read in the previous pages. Let it all settle in for a few moments before you proceed to the next chapters. While you are doing so, remember how much you are loved and treasured.

For this is who He is—the One who loves you above all else.

CHAPTER 8

Reason

There are several reasons why things are as they are. They may be as they are because we choose them to be that way. They may be because another has created a situation that affects us through our relationship with them. They may be because it's the way it is.

This last statement may have you puzzled, as I was the first time I was introduced to it. Does this mean we have no control over the events of our life, the situations that come to us? We have no choices to make?

No, this is not what it means. It simply means forces that surround us may affect us in ways that we are not always aware of or have learned to protect ourselves against. Let me give you an example.

You are walking down the street and come across someone who sneezes into the crowd where you are. The sneeze is full of bacteria that are sprayed into the environment. You may not be aware of the actual sneeze, but you are the unwilling recipient of the bacteria. You may also become ill from those bacteria. You can do little to control the situation. It is just the way it is.

You can, however, learn to connect in such a way as to keep your energy field free of that energy which "attracts" negative forces. We stated before that energy gives and receives and attracts that which is like it. In staying within the positive light of God's pure love, the true energy force, you can create a protective shield, so to speak, to keep you healthy and balanced. Remember, within His pure love comes abundance and, with your gift of free will, of choice, you can experience this abundance.

Am I saying we can keep our physical bodies free of contaminants, illnesses and diseases? To a very large extent, yes, we can. Of course, genetics, chemical and environmental factors also play a part, but we can help control the effects of all these and more from attacking and destroying our bodies. The pure energy that is created from His love, and our self-love that is connected to Him, can protect the energy field that surrounds us and keep our body systems balanced and whole. This balance and wholeness allows the positive response of harmony within us that can only produce the state of well-being in all dimensions, including the physical.

You may be wondering just what happens to free will and choice when something "bad" happens, such as a car wreck or a rape or murder. We do not make the decision for these to happen to us. It is not a matter of placing ourselves in particular situations for horrendous things to happen to us. Are these other examples of happenings that occur just because they occur? Can it be said they are the result of "randomness" rather than for a reason? I think not. Let me explain.

Randomness suggests no rhyme or reason behind these occurrences; however, everything in the universe has a spark of divinity in its being or it would not be. With God, since all is of His world, His creation, there is reason in everything.

You may be asking yourself, where is the spark of divinity in the case of rape or murder? Did God create these horrible things? It would be very hard to explain to the victim that it was an act of God and, of course, it wasn't. It was an act of man exercising his gift of free will. So, where exactly is the divinity in this painful situation?

It is in the knowing that God is with us at all times and with Him, we will find a way to handle, through His love, what comes into our life. He is the stabilizing force that feeds us strength, power and courage to see our way through and grow into our essence with any situation. He did not create the horrors that man forces on other men, but He is there to help pick up the pieces of our life and make it whole again. This is where the divinity is. This is the reason.

Let's explore a rape situation. God gave each participant, the rapist and the victim, free will. He was with the rapist in the moments of decision-making to commit the crime. He was the voice of love and healing, but His voice was not heard. The rapist went on, through his free will, to create his violence upon his victim.

The victim was an innocent individual who suffered the result of the rapist's free will and horrible decision. She is now part of his creation and her life has been affected by it. It is part of her world and the way it is. She did not choose this to happen to her, so where is her free will in this?

Now enters the complexity in understanding, but even in this, He is with us. She did not choose by any means or any definition of free will for this act to be forced upon her. So was she a "random" choice by the rapist or not? Was she "in the wrong place" when he was ready to strike? No. Certainly it was very unfortunate that he singled her out, but it was as it was to be and it was to be because he made it so. Did she choose the act of rape? No. Did she choose any other act of violence? No. Did she choose this particular situation? No. She was, however, now connected to him, his energy, and his creation, through his inability to hear and love. He now made his—and her—experience.

Remember our earlier discussion on the reason we are here in this life—to learn love and to experience ways in which to do this, the ways in which our spirit can grow and become one with God? She did not choose to be a rape victim, but now she has the opportunity, the experience, which can allow her to learn love and achieve higher spiritual awareness. The event assaulted her body, but now can fuel her soul and spirit with God's grace and love to grow into oneness with Him if she accepts it. This is the reason. This is the reason for all that is in the universe. This is the only reason.

It is true she did not have the chance to exercise her gift of free will to prevent this from coming into her life. It is true the rapist's free will created her reality. It is true she has to renew her body and spirit with healing and now, it is only her free will that can do this. Now is her chance to seek Him and His grace and His love to mend the shattering of her life. Now, this is the reason.

God did not create the horrors of man, but He did create the means in which to heal when His gift of free will is abused. His creations are of love and beauty and wholeness. They are powerful and strong enough to overcome any abuses by man if we choose to call upon them and give our cry, our life, ourselves to Him. This is the reason.

Randomness, no. Always, always, reason.

Okay, what about my statement that we choose things to be the way they are. Why indeed would we choose to be sick, physically, mentally, emotionally or spiritually? The choice may be conscious or not, but the answer is simply to learn.

As I stated previously, our purpose here is to learn to love and we all have a way in which we are to do this, our own special way. The way may involve experiencing certain life situations that another may not experience. Our pathway through the situation determines, by the choices we make, the love we surround ourselves with, and the asking for help from the Higher Power, how we progress through it. Some continue to struggle long past that which is necessary in order to learn what it is they are to learn. Some just never seem to "get it". Some never let love into their lives, the kind of love that heals. So the choices destroy rather than heal.

See? We are back to healing. Full circle. Love is necessary to heal. Healing cannot take place without it.

Again, He is love.

CHAPTER 9

Essence

We saw in the rape story how another can create a situation that affects us. Our own story may not be as dramatic, but everyday events can impact us. The secret is not to let it. Oh, sure. Easier said than done, right? Yes, but it can be done. How? By remembering our essence, by remembering our core—our soul and our spirit. If we give them up to others, by their demands, by their frustrations, by their control, by their anger and fear, we give up the very center of our being. We are lost totally. We have surrendered ourselves to their essence.

Now that is a powerful statement—"surrendered ourselves to their essence".

What about the belief that all essence was good, was generous, and was loving? After all, it is the spirit we are talking about. How could it not be good? Well, it is possible for the spirit to be, by choice, void of love, of caring, of truth, of the power of the Spirit. Is this where you wish your essence to be placed? I think not.

We may not be able to control whether someone in our life is involved in an accident and is terribly hurt, or experiencing a terminal illness, nor prevent the suffering of a loved one. These can and do happen and we must give of ourselves to them. But giving does not involve or demand that we lose who we are in the process; for the most precious gift God has given us is self-love. Remember, we are His total creation in His image. This makes us the most precious of all creation to Him. If we are this special to Him, this treasured by Him, this source of His joy, then we must love ourselves first as our gift back to Him. Therefore, we must love and protect our essence. I must say here, loving ourselves does not mean selfish, self-centered love. It means the kind of love that comes from the pure love of God. It is a love that is wrapped in warmth and caring and protection of the core of us. It is a love that generates love, not harbors it.

If we do not love ourselves, how can we love others? If we do not give to ourselves, how can we give to others? If we do not protect ourselves, how do we protect others? If we cannot do these things, what happens to the world around us? Remember, we are all connected. We are all one. What we do to ourselves, we do to all. Think about this for just a moment—what we do to ourselves, we do to all. A most powerful statement, don't you think? This is the power of us. This is how strong a force we generate. This is who we are. This is essence.

Do you know your essence? Are you protecting it or are you surrrendering it to others? Does it need healing to bring you to that place of self-love, to the knowing that your essence is His essence?

We are back to healing. Healing. With it comes power, creation, force, truth, comfort, peace, strength, honesty, joy, happiness, oneness, unity, essence and, most of all, love. Healing is a gift of our creation from His love.

Do you see a pattern here? It speaks of life and love, creation and oneness, essence and healing force—and it speaks of God.

He is all of these.

CHAPTER 10

Healing Ways

Healing is so important to our understanding of who we are that I must continue in this discussion.

I spoke earlier of healing—both of oneself and others—and I spoke in a very limited way of my experience with healing. I would like to share more so you may have a better understanding of the nature of healing.

Through my introduction with Reiki, I experienced first hand the power of the Spirit. As I said before, the nature of the method of healing is not what is important. What is key is invoking the Highest Spirit, God, to aid in the healing and to unite with Him through love. I felt the power of this love with my attunement to Reiki. It was a force so powerful and complete and total it was infused in my total being. It generated emotion so strong and sure I was overcome to the point of tears. It was a wondrous journey into wholeness and oneness with Him such as I had never known.

Just what happened? During Reiki attunement, which is a process of initiation to full connection, the Spirit is called upon to join with the spirit of the one receiving the attunement. This unity of spirits is joyous and complete. It actually can be felt physically as well as emotionally. It is a union that generates a force that can be hot or cold, electric or calming, and much more, but it is always pure and complete.

For me, it was a sensation of energy coming into my being with such force I felt it radiating throughout every inch of my body. It sent energy waves through me, immediately bringing me to tears. The emotion that He generated is something I have trouble explaining. I can only ask you to think of a moment when you were so overcome with emotion it left you breathless and unable to speak and then magnify this a million times and you may begin to know what I felt. It was always the same with subsequent attunements to the advanced Reiki levels I attained. There was always the force of His presence, the beauty of His presence, the wonder of His presence and, always, always the joy.

I also received with the attunement the understanding that, with His presence, we have the ability to heal. This may seem an extreme statement to some of you, but it is true. You see, we put limits on ourselves because we do not fully understand the power of our connection with God. We must always remember we are His creation and we are created as He is. He has the power to heal; therefore, we have the power to heal. And we heal through the forces that connect us all, those of love and energy.

The easiest way to heal is through the physical way is which we can connect with every other life form every single day of our life. It is through our sense of touch. We touch all day long. This is the medium we use every day and night to connect. So too, it is with healing. Our hands carry with them the most powerful physical way to connect for healing. We can learn to feel the energy that surrounds us and we can generate the love force within us and transmit it to all of life. Let's try a simple experiment.

Rub your two hands together for a few seconds. Now separate your hands to a few inches apart from each other and slowly bring them together, without touching. Try a few more inches, moving them slowly in and out from each other. Do you feel a "pressure" between them? It is as if there is an invisible wall that keeps them apart. This is the energy field that surrounds them and is the same as the energy that surrounds the entire body, the energy that is connected to others. Through this energy field, healing can occur. The hands do not have to actually touch the person receiving healing, though that is fine. What is important is connecting to the energy of that person and bringing in the love force. The hands are the vessel; but the intention to heal through love is how the healing is transmitted.

Love again is the key. Without it, healing cannot occur. A true healer incorporates this love into his or her healing practice, the practice of bringing higher good to the receiver. Higher good. Does that necessarily mean physical cure? Physical perfection? Physical good health? No. It means healing in whatever way is best for that being. Let's explore this.

We all experience challenges on many different levels. I do not say we "suffer" for we do not have to. I say rather, we "experience". All of our experiences are different from those of another. This is for purpose, our purpose to learn love. Our experience may be a physical one, but it may also be mental, emotional or spiritual.

We must not confuse "healing" with "cure". Cure speaks of medical intervention resulting in a dramatic change to the physical body. However, healing speaks of higher good. And higher good may be for higher awareness in mental, emotional or spiritual states. It may have nothing to do with the physical body. A true healer knows this. He or she knows when healing is given it is for specific purpose, with the unity of God, for higher good. Does this mean physical healing is not also received? Not necessarily. Remember, it is for higher good and the higher good for that person may be physical healing. Healing goes where it is needed. For those of you who may want concrete "proof" found in a lab or medical test or x-ray, you may be disappointed. Healing of a much more glorious and wonderful kind may have been received and that you cannot measure.

Healing for the higher good of a life force is what I

have been called to do as part of my purpose in this lifetime. Calling in the Highest Spirit, God, and uniting with Him in love, generates a healing connection which is transmitted through me for higher awareness of that being, higher awareness in any dimension needed by that being. It is created by Him, and through our connection, heals. So it is with others called to be healers for His purpose.

My experience with healing also has led to an understanding of the self-healing that I spoke of earlier. I have known this dramatically. Once again, healing comes from love and self-love is the greatest gift we have been given. In loving ourselves, we love our Creator. This makes perfect sense doesn't it? Because we are one, there is no separation between us. God=Self=One. When we ask for the power of our union with Him and feel the love of Him and the self-love, we can be healed.

In feeling the total union with my Creator and in knowing His love for me and mine for Him and in giving my spirit complete oneness with Him, I have been healed. This is a powerful statement, and this journey has taken me on several paths, all at various speeds and distances, but all leading me to Him. It has been a most powerful, awesome and wondrous experience. It can be the same for you if you open yourself to it.

For this is who He is. Powerful. Awesome. Wondrous.

The journey continues.

CHAPTER 11

Oneness

I had a lump in my breast that was present for several years. It was required of me by my doctor to have regular exams by him and a surgeon yearly. I had mammograms and ultrasounds done. I had biopsies done to determine its pathology. Now, the lump is no longer present. It is gone.

I experienced the pain and fatigue of Fibromyalgia, which is a muscular and sleep disorder, for more years than I care to remember. It caused pain in my trunk, joints and extremities to the point where it was uncomfortable even to wear clothes. The pressure of the weight of the clothing caused pain. It limited my motor movements and restricted my activity. It took a great deal of determination daily to work through the pain and sleepiness in order to do what I had to do to complete my obligations both personally and professionally. Now, the pain and fatigue of this disorder are gone.

You may doubt my statement that I have been healed, but it is true. I did not have any medical intervention to "cure" these conditions. Medicine was not able to affect these changes. How then did they occur?

In saying I was healed, I mean I opened myself up to the floodgates of love from other healers, my guides and angels and of the Supreme Being, God. Remember, love is necessary for healing. It is impossible without it.

Remember also that self-love is the beginning of all love. In my search for truth, I was able to love myself completely, as the creation of the Spirit. I was able to love myself as He loves me. This is important to remember. We are connected, He and I. No separation. In loving me, I love Him. So too, it is for you. You and He are connected. No separation. In loving yourself, you love Him. This is a most beautiful state.

My healing began when I was able to open myself up to this love. I was then able to feel His presence, His power and His truth—the truth that He loves all of His creation with every fiber and strength of His being. In accepting our essence and our need for Him, we open ourselves to His abundance, the abundance that He desires for all of us. Healing is but a part of that abundance. When I realized my body was His creation and it was created from His love, I asked for my healing, through His love. I knew of higher purpose by then. I knew of energy. I knew of connectedness. I knew of oneness and I knew of His love.

Would my healing be possible without my asking or without other healers asking for me? Would it be possible without opening myself to His love? Would it be possible without our connectedness? No, very simply, no, for again, and always, healing is about love. Love of self, love of others and love of the Creator. If I had not learned to love and care for myself as I was, then I would not have asked. If I had not asked, it would not have been given to me. This is a key point to know. We must ask for what it is we desire. We must seek Him and lay our desires, wants, truths, hopes and pleasures in His presence. Understand this.

Everything we are is of, by and from Him, our

Creator. Everything we have or seek or need or desire is His pleasure to give us. We can never have too much or be too much or dream too much or desire too much. For He, as our Father/Mother/All, wants everything for us. This includes our healing, on whatever level we need it, in order to fulfill our purpose and learn our way to love. All—everything—comes back to, and is, love. Everything.

In understanding this, I opened myself to my healing. I have energy and strength as I never had before. I am able to maintain a healthy weight and I exercise to maintain fitness. I was not able to do this before. My physical healing is the direct result of love, for myself and for my Creator.

My healing was not only that of my physical body. It was also, and most joyously, healing of my spirit. I received healing in the most complete and grandest way possible—union of my spirit with His. Again, in finding my essence and my connectedness with my Creator, I found the union that made me complete, made me whole. This wholeness brought into my life happiness and peace and a joy that tends to made me want to burst from the power of it. It is hard for me to contain it at times; then again, why must it be contained? It is the joy of God.

Did this healing occur without challenge, without struggle, without doubt and question? No. Was my faith and trust not put to test? It absolutely was. But the most important thing to remember is—I had felt the energy of His love. I had felt the power of His love. I had felt His presence. I had felt His truth. No matter how I sought and struggled, I did not want to be separated from those feelings. Yes, there were times I questioned if I would ever understand, ever know and yes, there were times I was tempted to give up the struggle, but I could not. For His love always called me back. He never left me alone without it.

Why was this? Why did He not give up on me? Why did He not say I would never understand? Why did He not throw up His hands in exasperation and shake His head at my struggle? Because He heard my cry of pain and He was answering it. From His love, He was answering it. From that moment of my reaching to Him, He was bound to me totally, completely, without reservation or question. We were one.

He is this, also. Our answer. Our truth. Our bond.

CHAPTER 12

The Puzzle

My struggle. Yes, you can believe it. I did struggle. It was much harder than it needed to be, this healing of mine. I did not know it at the time, but I do now. Now I understand what it was that made it so hard. Now I know what would have made it so, so simple. I hope you can learn from my experience, which is why I am writing these pages.

One very, very simple step which causes so much grief, frustration, unhappiness and pain, is—not giving our cry to Him. We too often do not do this. What exactly does it mean, you may be asking?

Our cry may be one of wants or desires or needs or hopes. It may be of pain or anger or fear or hopelessness or loneliness. It may stem from our hurts and aches in our hearts and souls. Whatever it is, it is our cry. It is what separates us from peace and joy. In giving our cry to Him, and trusting it is cherished and protected, we are giving ourselves to Him. There is no better place to be. It is the best place in the universe. Just think of it—you have given your cry to Him. He has taken it. He is cherishing and treasuring it. He is protecting it. He values it as the most precious thing in the universe. Feel this. Feel what this means. Feel.

Imagine your most valued treasure in your hands, be it your spouse, child, pet or other loved one, or a material object. Whatever it is, imagine it in the warm, loving caress of your hands. Feel what it means to you. Feel what it generates in you. Feel the strength of it. Feel its power to make you feel. Feel it all. Now take that feeling and magnify it to the ends of the Earth and you still cannot imagine the degree of His feeling for your cry. It is His most precious treasure.

Now imagine, in the depths of His feeling for you and your treasure, what He would do to care for it, to love it. Can we imagine it? Do we even have this capability? I wonder. We know how we would care for our treasure, how we would protect it, how we would value it. And, yet, we are not the Creator. As the Creator, He has the capacity to safeguard our treasure and to make it whole as we cannot. In all that He is, what better place is there for us to be? None.

We know this now. So, then, what is the problem? Why do we struggle? Why do we continually challenge ourselves? These are tough questions, but the answer is simple. It is because we do not leave our cry, our treasure, with Him. We keep taking it back. We let our humanness, our ego, our truth get in the way. We think we know how things "should" be. We think we have the answers. We think our truth is greater than His. We think we know how all the pieces of our life fit together. Well, my friends, I have found we do not know. We know only a very, very limited piece of our world, certainly not enough to even begin to put a few pieces together. But He knows it all. He is the one fitting it all together. Only He can do this.

The secret in learning the puzzle of our life is simple. It is to listen. He is willing, in fact, is most anxious to share what He knows with us. In stilling ourselves and opening to His essence connecting with ours, we will hear His voice. We will know what we are about. We will know our purpose. We will know who we are. We will know we have everything we need to be. We will know He will bear the weight of our life for us.

We struggle because we choose to struggle. Our challenges are ours because we make them ours. Our path is hard because we make it hard. Harsh statements, aren't they? But they are true. Every time we take back our cry, it is our choice. It is our choice to bear the weight by ourselves.

He does not want difficulty for us, or pain or sorrow. He wants joy, happiness, laughter and radiance for us. And He will give us all these and more.

For this too, He is. Joy. Happiness. Laughter. Radiance.

CHAPTER 13

Perfection

Joy. Happiness. Laughter. Radiance. This and more He will give to us if we give Him our life. "Give Him our life", another powerful statement. Let's explore it.

In understanding our connectedness, it is easy to accept that we are nothing without Him. What may come as a shock and often with much resistance and denial is—He is nothing without us. Wow! Not how you pictured God, huh? But think about it. He made us in His image and we need Him. Doesn't it follow then that He needs us also? We need Him to be one. Doesn't He need us to be one? Remember the two bodies of water we spoke of earlier coming together as one? No separation between them? No defining one from another? We are the same as those bodies of water. We need each other to be one.

In giving Him our cry—whatever it is—we give ourselves to Him. In this giving, we are showing Him our understanding of our connectedness. He needs this. He needs to be one with us. He cannot "take" what we are not ready to give, and if we cannot give, it keeps us separate. So His need is as great as ours. We are what makes Him whole, makes Him complete, and makes Him connected to us. He longs to hear from us because He longs for unity with us. He is alone and lonely without us. Give Him your cry. Make Him whole.

Does it strike you as bold for me to say He is not whole unless we make Him so? We must look back to the idea of our creation to understand. We are made as He is. We are the mirror image of Him. We need Him to be whole; He needs us to be whole. We must not make Him so untouchable, so foreign, so unlike us to keep us separate. Too many of us believe He is so much more than we are, so unattainable, so different we can't believe we are the same as He is. We need only to remember—we are made as He is.

We also believe that only in valuing our picture of Him are we honoring Him. Many of us have been indoctrinated from our religious upbringings to have a picture of Him that does not allow any variance from it and it is this picture that keeps us away from Him. It is one that deigns to make Him so holy, so divine, so supreme and sovereign we come to view Him as a being only unto Himself. We feel we are disrespectful or we are dishonoring Him if we admit to our sameness, our oneness. We cannot imagine we do have or can have the same power as He does, the same force He has, or the same love He has. We must learn to view this differently.

All was given to us at the time of our creation. It is only in recognizing, no, it is only in accepting this fact that we give honor to Him. It is in knowing our complete and total perfection, as He is perfect, that we are respecting Him. As His image, we are the same. This was His gift to us with our creation. We must not diminish Him by our inability to perceive Him as He is. We must not limit Him, which is exactly what we are doing, when we do not accept. He created us through love; so it can be said, in not accepting our total likeness and all that it is, we are not accepting His love.

Some of you may have a problem with me stating we are perfect as He is perfect. We have only to look at our physical bodies to know this is not true. We have only to look at the errors of judgment, the "mistakes" we make, and the imperfections in our moods, behaviors and emotions to know this is not true. What am I speaking of?

The perfection I am relating to is the perfection of our soul and total spirit. This is how we connect with His spirit. This is the absolute and total image likeness we share with Him. We are perfect in soul and total spirit because He has made it so. This was His plan—to create that essence of us which goes on and on, knowing only His love and joy, and which time, space and distance does not interfere. The essence—our soul and total spirit—is the perfection of the universe. He is the Creator of the universe and the essence of all in it is His perfection. This is another gift of our creation—perfection.

In knowing this, we can move to greater heights of awareness, greater levels of who we are. For in knowing our soul and spirit perfection, we do not limit ourselves to only that which we know consciously or concretely. We truly are able to "become" as He intended—connected to His spirit and His perfection. He does not stand alone. He needs us to be and we need Him to be. "Becoming" is acceptance of our sameness, our likeness, and our essence as one with His.

I said earlier, in giving Him our cry, we give Him ourselves. In giving ourselves, we give our life. Do you understand this? Our cry comes from the depth of us. It comes from the essence of who we are. It is the place where we as spirits live. It is from our heart and soul. Our heart and soul make us who we are and who we are is life. Life is what is connected to Him for He is our Creator. Therefore, in giving Him ourselves, through our cry, we give Him our life. Once we have done this, truly given Him our life, we are accepting all that He is. For we would not give ourselves to someone or something we did not accept, would we? Would we give our treasure, our most valued treasure, to that which we did not know or trust or honor or believe in? I think not.

Curious then why it is so hard for us to give our life to Him, isn't it? We cry, we ask, we seek, we beg, we plea, we bargain, but all we have to do is give. In the giving, we have all we will ever need. Knowing and accepting this brings the freedom to receive the abundance. How does this work?

Giving ourselves allows Him to fulfill His need—His need for us, His need to be connected, as we have already discussed. It also allows Him to then give to us. We've said He cannot take what we are not ready to give. Well, He also cannot give what we are not ready to receive.

Connectedness takes more than one. One cannot be connected to itself; it must be connected to something or someone else. It is the same with us and with Him. What can He be connected to if not us, His creation? He creates. We are the same as He is. United. Unity means oneness. Oneness means same. Same means whole. Whole means complete. Complete means us. He and His creation—full circle.

Do you see? Do you see the importance of giving Him our life? Our life to Him fully and completely is the most precious gift we can give Him; for we are giving Him back Himself. Remember, there is no separation. In recognizing we are the same and in giving our life to Him, we are recognizing the magnificence of who He is. How is this so?

Just as we have said earlier, same means whole. If our life is our most precious treasure, and we give it to

Him, we are acknowledging our need for wholeness. We have given it to the one, the only one, who can make us whole. We know this; otherwise, we would not have turned to Him in the first place. Is this not magnificent? This is all we have to do—turn to Him for wholeness. He will handle all the details of our life. He will solve the puzzle. Only one who is magnificent can do this.

Whole. Complete. Same. Magnificent. These too, are who He is.

CHAPTER 14

Love

Love. Where do I begin to tell you of love? The scope of love is so vast, how can I encompass all that it is on these pages? And how in the world do I even begin to explain the love of the Spirit? I trust He will give me the words. I know He will give you the feeling if you let Him.

Joy. Radiance. Happiness. Abundance. Glory. Power. Eternal. Complete. Total. Whole. Perfect. Wondrous. Life. These, and much more, barely touch on all that love is. It can make us weep, grieve, feel loss and pain at the same time it fills our hearts and spirits with healing. It is the life force. It is all we will ever need to live, to survive, to be who we are to be and to be one with our Creator.

It seems there are no perfect words to communicate what it is, which has been the problem for poets and writers since the beginning of time. This is because it is felt, and how does one explain a feeling? Love must be known to our core for understanding. Feelings and emotions are to be lived, not put on paper. So, again I ask, how do I tell you of love? How, indeed? I cannot, but He can. Not only can He, but He will. It takes only one thing—for you to open your heart to His.

We are back to asking. Remember in the beginning I told you our exploration of God starts with asking Him who He is? Well, so it is with His love. We can know He loves us from our teachings by our parents, churches and schools, but we cannot experience it unless we are ready to receive it from Him. He is ever ready to give it, but again, He will not force us to take it. We must ask for the experience of it. We must ask for the knowing of it. We must ask. It is only in the asking that He can give it completely. We also said He needs us as we need Him. He needs for us to reach to

Him and His love before He can give all He has to give. This is who He is. This is when He can bless us with all in His universe.

This is how my healing came to be. This is how I have felt His oneness with me. This is how He has blessed my life with abundance. This is how I have received total communion with Him, by asking Him into my life. Did I know His love before my cry of pain? To a point, I did. What I did not know was the extent of His love for me. Now I can feel His arms around me in protection and caring and warmth and trust. Now I know of His presence. Now I can *feel* Him. There are no words to tell you, so I am tempted to end this chapter here, but my heart wants you to feel Him also.

Let's try something. Imagine you are in a boat lost at sea. You are alone. Nothing but wave after wave of endless water surrounds you. The sun beats down on you during the day and you feel the damp cold penetrate you to the bone at night. You are hungry and thirsty and afraid. You despair. Close your eyes and visualize this scene. Feel it.

Now imagine again. You have spotted a shape of something out on the horizon. You are afraid to even hope it is a ship. But as it gets closer, you can see that it is. You are joyous and full of hope. Alas, you have no way of making it aware of you and it passes you by. You are again alone. Close your eyes and visualize this scene. Feel it.

You continue to remain at sea, lost. You are barely able to hang on now. Your skin is sunburned, your lips are chapped and waves continue to make you seasick. You are weak. No one hears your barely audible plea for help. Imagine the remote possibility of being rescued, of being seen again in that vast expanse of water. Feel your despair, your hopelessness and your anguish. Feel it.

Now, hope reigns again. Another sighting of a ship and this time, you are seen! You are the complete and total focus of all activity on that ship. You are the center of its world. You are all it is about. You are one with it and all that it is. You. Imagine it—a huge, wonderful, powerful force focusing totally on you. All the caring and concern and rescue are for you.

How do you feel? What emotion is stirring in you right now? Has your anguish turned to hope? Your fear to relief? Your pain to joy? Your restlessness to peace? Your sadness to happiness? Your despair to gladness? Your emptiness to fullness? Your fatigue to wonder? Your weakness to energy? Are you filled with all that is good and whole? All that is perfect and complete? Can you feel the excitement of that ship as it reaches toward you in rescue? Can you feel its energy? Can you feel the power of it?

You were lost at sea tired, hungry and thirsty. You drifted for days, no hope left in you. You suffered so. You anguished with no ear hearing your weakening voice. You were alone. Or were you? Was there presence with you? Was there hope even though you had to search for it? Was there rescue all along? Of course there was. You are never, ever alone.

But did you feel presence when I asked you to imagine those scenes? Was your focus on your fear and misery and loneliness? Was your focus on how hard you had it? Was your focus on your abandonment? Was your focus on your pain? This is what we do to ourselves. We focus on our feelings of what is outside of ourselves and not on what resides within. It is within that we are. It is within that we exist. It is within that we are one.

Compare the feelings in our "lost at sea" scenes with the "rescue scene". Compare the emotions. Do not continue to read on until you have done this, for this is where the knowing begins. This is where the understanding of love begins. The love is always there; you just have to ask for its oneness.

The power, the power of the ship reaching for you, no one else, just you, is magnificent. Total focus on you, total rescue of you, total oneness with you—this is what His love is about. Ask for Him, with all that you have, with all that you are. Ask for Him with the voice that may be barely audible. Ask for Him and turn your feelings of anguish, hopelessness, loss, loneliness and abandonment to the ones you experienced when you visualized your rescue. Ask, and He will reach for you.

Does this mean we can only reach for Him in our tough times, those times in which we come close to falling apart or when life beats us down? Absolutely not. He is with us at all the happy and joyous times of our life, too. But even they can be made better, if we wish to share them with Him. We forget this. We tend only to call on Him when we are struggling, when life's challenges are difficult for us. But we are missing out and He is missing out if we do not share each and every moment of the day with Him. He is one with us, remember? But again, He will not force us to take that which we are not ready to receive. If we are not ready to receive more, more joy, more happiness, more peace, more radiance, more abundance, He will not give them to us because we have not asked.

In the asking for Him, at all times of our life, He will give, give and give. This is love. This is what love is all about. Giving and receiving. Giving our life to Him and receiving His abundance. He receives the gift of our life, our love to Him, and He in turn gives His love and abundance to us. He gives, as we give. He receives, as we receive.

For this is who He is. Giving. Receiving. Loving.

CHAPTER 15

Free Will

We have talked of many things so far in our exploration of the Spirit. You have heard my words of love, oneness, hope, trust, giving, receiving, abundance, beauty, peace, joy, happiness, wonder and all glorious things that He is.

But I know you also question pain, hardship, loss, grief, darkness, despair, anger, hatred, fear, abandonment, loneliness and the imperfections of life and wonder where He is in all of these. How do all of these and more exist if there is this beautiful, giving, loving life force I have told you about? Why does the earth and all that it holds suffer so? Why do we kill and hate? Why do we go to war? Why do our children suffer? Why is there disease and illness? Why is there poverty and want? Why do some have and some do not? Why do the nations of the world not live in peace and harmony? Indeed, why do our neighbors not? Why is the cry of mothers not heard or that of the aged and infirmed? Why is the environment abused? Why do we not respect? Where is God in all of this mess? Well, friends, He is there, just as He is everywhere. He is there to help us. The thing we must understand is our creative power in all the mess.

One of the greatest gifts He has given us is free will. We have said He will not give until we are ready to receive. He also will not interfere with the choices we make through our will. He will watch and grieve for us. He will cry for our choices. They will sadden Him. He will wonder why we are not hearing His voice. He will want for us everything He has to give us. But He will not interfere.

With our creation, He blessed us with the gifts He Himself desired. For remember, as He is, we are. He did not desire to be dictated to. He did not desire to be told. He did not desire to be controlled. He desired freedom, freedom to be, the freedom of soul and spirit. So He gave us this gift— freedom.

With its giving however, also came responsibility; for He desired responsibility, too. We must remember this. We are soul of His soul, spirit of His spirit. We are one. As He is, we are. He respects our oneness, our wholeness and He will not detract from it. So, what does this have to do with pain, suffering and so on?

We see Him as the most powerful, loving force in the universe, which He is. However, we also have expectations that we impose on that force. We have created our image of Him that may or may not fit the reality of who He is. We make Him who we want Him to be. We desire life to be perfect. We desire a life free of hardship, pain or grief. We desire laughter, wealth, peace and harmony. And we *expect* Him to provide it. Deep down, we expect it.

So what do we do when life turns out differently than our expectations? We blame—we point the finger of blame. We rant and rave and turn against. We criticize and find fault. We must find someone or something to hold responsible. Too very often that someone or something is God. How in the world can He let these horrendous things happen to us? What did we ever do to Him to cause these hardships in our lives?

What injustice! What cruelty! What abandonment! Surely this was not meant for us or for our world! Why are we being punished? Why must we suffer? Why is this happening? We plead, "Please, God, *MAKE THIS STOP*! You *MUST* make this stop!"

What it is we have to learn is that God does not create hardship in our life. He does not wish us pain and suffering. He is not some malevolent force that decrees suffering on us. *WE MUST LOOK TO OURSELVES*. What are the choices we are making? What are we not hearing within ourselves? What are we not seeing or hearing from those around us? Are we coming from the point of fear and anger or love? Are we selfish, self-centered, controlling or loving? Are we full of that which eats us up—all the negative forces in the universe—or do we love?

As stated earlier, He will not interfere with our free will. Our choices may bring the greatest hardship we will ever have to face, but He will not interfere. In His love for us, He wants whatever it is we want. If we make a decision or a choice, then obviously it is because it is what we want. Makes perfect sense, doesn't it? So why would He interfere? Why would He decide *for* us rather than let us be whom He created—free beings? It is very important to Him to allow us to be who we are. Only in being who we are can we give to Him, be one with Him. It does not make sense then for Him to thwart our desires, our choices and decisions. He gives those to us to own. They are our responsibility. We made the decisions. We must learn to point the finger of blame at ourselves, for this is where it lies.

Whatever is happening in your life is of your creation. You have shaped and molded it. You have made it what it is, no one else. Certainly not God. It is true He will help you reshape or remold your creation; but it is not of His making. You and the power of your free will have made it what it is.

Now, you may ask, what of floods, hurricanes, avalanches, earthquakes and so on. Why does He *let* those occurrences happen? Why doesn't He stop them? He can prevent them and all would be well. Yes, it is true, He could prevent them, but why should He? They are forces of nature that are also of His creation and they are life. He respects all life for there is purpose in it. Just because we do not understand the purpose does not mean it is not to be or it is not to exist. It means simply it is as He has created it.

The fact the earth experiences changes in its natural forces that may wreak havoc on us does not mean

He is to stop them. Nature is as it is. It is allowed to be as it is. Just as you and I are allowed to be as we are. There is purpose in natural "disasters". Only we, not He, view them as "disasters". Since He created the forces that culminate in their power, He sees them only as natural processes with purpose. As with all life, purpose that creates change is the natural process of all life forces. Some of these changes we can see in our environment and some we cannot. But remember, all life has purpose. Just because it is not known to us or is not understood by us, is not the point. The only point we are to remember is—it is as He created it.

Do you have a problem with this idea? Does it strike you as selfish or lacking in compassion? I mean, really, if He knows the hardships and difficulties that will come about due to these "disasters", just how loving is He? Isn't this a contradiction? You may think so, but it isn't.

In order to understand, let's think about this scenario. You have just played a great game of tennis. Everything was perfect—your form, your energy level, your hitting, and so on. The result was, you won. Now, were just able to walk out on the court without ever having played before and been able to win that game? Absolutely not. You had to pay a price.

You had to get the equipment, learn the rules, learn the techniques and practice, practice and practice. You had to work hard to get the experience and skill and you had to be coached. Someone had to teach you. The purpose of the coaching was to teach you the game of tennis and to become a better you because of it.

So it is with "disasters". Remember we said purpose may or may not be seen? Might the purpose, or part of the purpose, be to allow us to be better because of experiencing all the "disaster" would teach us? Might it be to allow us to be "coached", to become more than we are now? Your tennis coach knew you may have hardship, struggle and disappointment in learning your new skill of the game, but he did not stop you from what you had to learn. He allowed you to do what it was you had to do to learn. He allowed you the experience of the process.

God knows you may have hardship, struggle and disappointment in learning to become the higher, better you. He also will not stop you from what you have to learn, from the process of becoming. He is caring enough, loving enough, to *let* you grow, to *let* you become, to *let* you be a higher you. Do you see it is not a contradiction? Do you see this still comes from the

Most High Creator out of love for us? In allowing us to experience, by our process of choice, free will and union with Him, He is allowing us to be the whole of our essence. It all comes from His love.

For more than anything else, this is who He is. Love.

CHAPTER 16

Dimensionality

Now we understand how we have an active part in the happenings of our lives due to the gift of free will and choice. But we also have some really, really tough questions to make sense of in our discovery of God.

What about physical handicaps, loved ones lingering through pain and suffering, children born with birth defects, disease, and on and on—where is He in this? Does He *let* these happen for us to become higher beings? This answer is not quite so easy to explain.

We are beings of many dimensions. We understand our physical dimension because it has been tested and explored and examined for centuries. We also have a very good understanding of our mental and emotional dimensions, although we still have much to learn of these. That part of us which is the most abstract and beautiful, however, we have comparatively little exploration. This is our spiritual dimension. It is also the most powerful.

How many of us tap into this power? How many even recognize it? If it is recognized, how many actually explore and develop it? It is a vista that is sadly neglected. We can go through our entire life and miss out on the most exquisite and glorious force that we have. Why do I say it is the most powerful? It is because it is our direct connection to God. Through this dimension, we have eternal life. Through this power, we have oneness. Through this power, we have the ability to transcend all the concreteness of our humanness, all the physical, mental and emotional awareness, and flow into and with His power. In connecting with His power, we become the essence of who we are.

This essence is spiritual. It is total spirit. It is the

part that elevates us to timelessness and a space that has no boundaries or limitations. It is the part of us that connects and leads us to greater and greater awareness of the entire universe and its dimensions. It is the part of us which creates, which defines who we are and which allows us to go far beyond the limits of our humanness to develop into higher and higher beings. It is the part of us that does not die.

Death, as we define it, is the permanent ending of life. This, however, speaks only of a physical death. The spirit does not die. The spirit goes on. In its transcendence from the earth plane to the universal energy, which is God, it finds peace and harmony with all the other life forces of His universe. It doesn't *then* become one with them, for it always was one with them. Rather, it is *aware* of its oneness. It is this awareness that is the force of the total—the complete—spirit.

Complete spirit? What is this about?

Spirit itself is multi-dimensional. It is, as we said, our connection to the universe. Our humanness however, imposes limitations. Our mental and emotional dimensions often seem to conflict with our spirit due to our need for logic and control. This need is not part of the spiritual dimension, however. We are free to be just spirit. We are rid of all the trappings that get in the way of being a truly free, complete spiritual life force. This freedom allows a pre-physical death dimension to become a greater post-physical death dimension. Since spirit is the connection to the life force—God—it is always searching for ways to develop its multi-dimensionality to become more and more. It desires to be more so it can be as close to the power of the Creator as possible. By tapping into the power of God, the spirit becomes greater. Remember we said we are created in His image? And remember who He is? He is perfection. Spirit desires this total image, this perfection, for in being as close to His perfection as possible, it is being as close to Him as possible.

It knows desire is not enough for perfection. It must grow into it. It knows also it is a choice to seek the higher state of perfection with Him. It knows it is given the chance to define its own state of development, once again because of free will. It "decides" then to experience states that allow it the opportunity for development.

Remember we said the spirit does not die? It lives on and on in eternity? It follows then, the dimensionality of the spirit must have the opportunity to develop to greater awareness in the eternal state, doesn't it? Well, this is so. We spoke earlier of guides and angels and these are examples of dimensionality of spirit. These are dimensions chosen by them for development, for continuation of their purpose for being.

There are also other ways for development through eternity, which brings us back to the original question. Does God *let* us experience hardship to develop into higher beings? The answer, which hopefully you have figured out by now, is—yes. Yes, absolutely. Why?—because our spirit has chosen it.

There are many ways to experience development. Some can be achieved only on the earth plane in physical human form and there are degrees to what one may choose to live in the search for higher awareness. Some ways are very "hard" from a human standpoint. Some are lifetime challenges. Some are easier than others. It is only in the experience that growing can be attained. Only in the growing can the perfection be attained. Complete spirit desires this growth for the continuation of its purpose of greater love for its Creator. It therefore, may choose to experience only that which can be experienced on the earth plane.

So, we are back to the original question. By making the choice, by exhibiting free will, spirit is allowed to live the choice of development. Spirit is allowed to experience the particular situation that will require growth. Spirit is allowed to experience physical handicap, or disease, or to linger in physical pain and suffering, because it is through this experience the dimensionality of perfection is attained.

It is all choice—the choice of the spirit. It is all love—the love of the Creator for each spirit and the love of each spirit for the Creator. It is all for the purpose of oneness and the perfection of the oneness.

He is this. Purpose. Perfection.

CHAPTER 17

Higher Dimension

I have said the spirit may chose to experience that which can only be experienced on the earth plane through the search for higher dimensionality. This infers the choice then to "return" to human existence from a different state of the spirit—the state of higher consciousness with God. Many refer to this state as "Heaven", but it is also called by other names. It is that existence which occurs after physical death. The return to human existence is often called "reincarnation". This may or may not be something you have believed in or even considered previously. If not, I ask you now to do so.

In order to come to a resolution or a place of comfort with this topic, let's go back to our earlier discussion, that is, our being created in His image. In our belief that God is all, everything, total and complete, this must include the ability to be able to incorporate many forms and states and energies. These are not limited to only one dimension, one power, and one presence. They encompass all matter of the universe, in all of its structure, and all of its oneness.

If this is our picture of the Most High in all of His power and glory, it follows then there are no limitations or restrictions on His being. Must it not also follow that we too have no limitations or restrictions on the states, forms or energies we can achieve since we are created in His image? Once again, we must not define Him according to that which we know, or rather, can be "proven" from a human level. He is much, much more than this.

There may be those of you reading this who feel

very uncomfortable with this notion of return from "beyond" to another human life, another experience in human form. It does make perfect sense, however, if we look at it from the viewpoint of our spirit, our essence. How can we limit it by only the earthly experience? How can we deign to say it is only that which we are comfortable with or "fits" into our perspective?

Spirit is multi-dimensional, as we have said, because it is the creation of the Most High Spirit. He did not create with limitation in mind. He created with pure love and power and with the desire to flourish it with the abundance of the universe. If this is so, abundance could not be given if it was limited from the start. To say spirit can only know one state or one form is to say He created with imperfection in mind. Imperfection is not who He is, therefore, we as spirit cannot be imperfect, as we are His image.

To transcend states, forms or energy is a gift He has given us. It allows us freedom to achieve our desires, to know oneness with all life and to be who it is we are striving to be. A limitation of process in only one state is saying He has decided for us all that we can be. Remember He has given us the gift of freedom. He does not make our choices for us. By making the choice to return as a human being, we are given the opportunity to "be" all that spirit is. It is through the human process we can accomplish higher awareness in a way that would not be possible in any other state.

We cannot achieve all spirit may choose to be in one lifetime. We may desire to be more, to reach higher states of awareness through our journey through eternity. Think about our definition of "eternity"—without end, forever, no ending. To believe spirit is content to remain with limitation in its awareness of Him for all eternity is incomprehensible. If spirit is His creation in His Image, through His love for abundance of all the universe, wouldn't it follow it would want to be more and more to His state of sameness? How can this be achieved if limitation was placed on it? I don't believe it can.

The human experience, with all of its challenges and situations, presents a field of opportunity to higher development. This is why a choice to return is made. In our journey of learning to love the Creator, self, others, and all life, we may "need" that which only the human lifetime can teach us. The "need" may be through a physical disability or disease or pain and suffering. It may be through being the parent of a sick child or the spouse of a suffering loved one. It may be through living the life of a "street person", or that of a drug addict or of being poor in an impoverished nation. It may be living the life of fame and fortune and its responsibilities. It may be as a world leader or common man. Whatever it is, it is our choice to experience in order to "become".

Now, you may look at those who have, in our eyes, drastically failed. We see those individuals such as Hitler or Jack the Ripper. We see those such as assassins or murderers. We see those who rob and cheat. We see those who are selfish and self-centered. How in the world are these people achieving higher awareness? Well, to be honest, they are not. They have misused their earthly experience, by their free will, not to learn love. They are still loved by the Creator because He loves all of His children, but the actions of these children are not loved. These are not of His creation. Remember He has given free will, but He also gave responsibility. In choosing the human experience, spirit accepts the responsibility that comes with it.

So what of these who do not learn what they have chosen to learn? What of their journey into higher awareness? What of those who do learn and wish to learn even more? Again, eternity is endless and any time through this journey is the opportunity to once more desire higher development and, in His love, return to human form and earthly state is given. He is most generous in allowing us our pursuit of perfection with Him. His generosity allows us to transcend one state to another, to experience His entire universe, and all of His creation as His image. His love allows Him to be generous.

For this He is. Generous.

CHAPTER 18

Choice

There is still much to discuss in our discovery of who God is. He is complex, but He longs for us to know Him and is willing to share all He can for our knowledge.

In His complexity, our understanding of Him may be so challenging to us in our limitations as human beings, we often give up in our knowing of Him. We begin to feel frustrated and lonely or abandoned. We begin to feel He is contradictory and unfair. We begin to feel we do not have the strength to hold on to faith and trust long enough to make sense of His message. In effect, we give up. We give up on the oneness He wishes us to have.

So, just how do we "hang on"? What is it we have deep inside us to give us the strength, the endurance, the courage and the trust to continue to seek Him? The answer is really very, very simple—we have His love. The problem is, we often don't know we have His love. We haven't allowed ourselves the opportunity to experience it, to know it. I must tell you from my own life, it is the most powerful force ever to be experienced. It is all we need for our existence. It is our life force.

So the question arises—if we do not have the strength and trust to hold on long enough to experience His love, how do we ever find it? If we give up before we feel it, how can we ever know it? Good questions, huh? Not so simple answers, but let's try.

In order to say we know something we first must experience it, right? We understand. We have knowledge of it. We make it our own. In order to know His love then, we feel we must dramatically experience it. Or do we? Must we first have conscious knowledge of it before it can be known? Must we have a "life-altering" experience before we say we know His love? I don't believe so.

How many times have you felt happy or found pleasure in the circumstances of your life? How many times have you rejoiced in the beauty of nature or the good fortune of yourself or loved ones? How many times have you considered yourself truly "lucky" or blessed with the abundance of your life? How many times have you been greeted with a smile or hug or a compliment? How many times have you been thankful you and your family are safe and well? How many times have you found more and more to treasure in your life? These questions can go on and on. Can you possibly consider them and still be able to say you have not experienced His love? Do you not know all of this and more is from His love? Do you not then have knowledge of His love?

We are so concrete. We are so ego-centered we wish to define the parameters of His love. We wish to fit Him into a context we are comfortable with. This is exactly where we make our mistake. We do not allow Him total expression of all He is. We give up on Him, as He would never do with us.

In our definition of our expectations of Him, we get caught up in the voices of our head. "Why doesn't this happen in my life?" "Why can't I be happy, rich, healthy, beautiful?" "Why do I have to suffer?" "Why can't I have all I want?" On and on it goes.

Then, we trap ourselves. The other voices start—"Please, God, give it to me now." "God, can't you hear me? Why don't you answer me?" or, "You said you would listen. You said all I had to do is ask. Well, I'm asking—now when do I get what I want?" We have decided our parameters. We have decided on the only answer we will accept. We make the choice to listen to our head and not our heart. We are giving up when the head speaks. We give up when the answer is not the one we want. We give up. We start to withdraw from our knowing Him. We will just show Him, won't we? If He will not give us what it is we have asked for, in our definition of what that is, then who needs Him anyway? Who the heck needs Him?

Big mistake. We are powerless without Him. The answer will not be found if we choose not to listen. The answers are always in our hearts and in our inner selves—not in the logic and concreteness of our heads. Head=humanness. Humanness=unknowing. Heart=spirit. Spirit=connection. Connection=Him. This formula is the key to success in our life. This formula will lead us to all the knowing we will ever need.

The one main ingredient missing in our head is the most important force in all creation—love. It is love that brings us the joy and peace in knowing. It is love that brings us unity and abundance. It is love that is our connection to the Source. It is love that He is.

Many feel the only experience of God is that which is presented in a graphic and dramatic way, such as a "miracle", or a near-death experience, or a wondrous intervention that saved a life, or prevented a "disaster", or that which is seen or read about in relation to another person. This is not so. In learning to look at our life—all of our life—and at the world around us, we can find Him anywhere, at all times, in all situations.

We tend though to take so much for granted. We often don't even take the time to view our life and all the blessings in it and give thanks. We do not see His hand in our life. We do not give Him credit for His participation. We seek Him only when we are in crisis and need. Not only do we not seek Him, we daily assure ways to prevent us from knowing Him.

We tend to use language that defeats us. We speak of the difficulties, the hardships, and the challenges. We bring failure to ourselves by our words. "I knew it would be hard." "Life can be so difficult." "That's just the way it is; I can't change it." We do not see He will help us.

We tend to accept defeat. We allow others and circumstances which enter our life to take us over. We give them our power. Yes, things happen. But we have the power to respond in such a way that allows us to rise above those things and control our response to them. Yet, we do not allow Him in to give us that power.

We tend to push others out of our life. We desire control. We desire the events of our life to be the way we want them and we selfishly "take charge" and other's opinions, desires and needs are of little importance to us. We do not allow love, His gift to us, to be the "controller" in our life.

We tend to subject ourselves to forces that deplete our energy and sap our strength. TV, movies and newspapers depict violence, crime, and destruction and man's inhumanity to man. We foster support for these negative influences by our attendance and attention. We do not see He could help us eliminate these forces from our world—energies of greed, corruption, abuse, lawlessness; energies of hate, fear, anger, frustration; energies of neglect, hunger, want and selfish pleasure. We do not see that His hand in ours, as one force, could rid our society of these energies.

We tend to object to the voices that present alternative choices to us: those who wish to protect our environment; those who speak of reform in our world governments; those who wish to protect the homeless, the mentally ill, the elderly, and the children; and those who speak of unity and oneness of purpose in fighting hunger, disease and need throughout our world. We do not allow His voice in to help us hear.

We tend to lash out at those who believe other than what we believe. We limit our outlook to incorporate only those creeds, ideals, principles and standards that are in our nature, upbringing or position in life. We judge others by their beliefs, color, sexuality, gender, and appearance. We value only that which is the same as we are. We do not see all as His children.

We tend to focus on that which we are unhappy about and feel sorry for ourselves. We often have our own little "pity party" and enjoy our misery and we are often not content to keep our pity to ourselves; we go out of our way to pull others into it. Our motto becomes "Misery Loves Company" and we relish in it. We do not see Him as our source of joy and happiness and "party" with Him.

We tend to believe our health, wealth, relationships, careers, family life, and social position are controlled by outside forces. We see hereditary and aging as blame for our physical condition. We see our employer and income as blame for our financial position. We see "she" or "he" and lack of understanding for blame for an unsatisfactory relationship. We see our co-workers, boss and administration for our discontent with our employment. We see our spouse or in-laws or troubled children as blame for our unhappy home. We see our neighbors and society as blame for where we live and play. We do not see we have the power to change, as creations of His image, any or all of this.

How can we know Him if we continue over and over again to push Him out of our life? How is it possible to experience Him if we continue to limit ourselves to our humanness? How can we possibly be all we can be without letting Him into our life? How can we believe our life could be different if we don't allow Him union with us? How is it possible? Most important, how can we be anything without His love?

The earth does not have to shake. The angels do not have to appear. The "Heavens" do not have to open up. The earth-shattering "miracles" of life do not have to occur. These are not necessary for you to know Him. These are not necessary for you to experience Him. Experience and knowing are everyday in every way in every moment. Examine your life and your world. Open your eyes—see His presence. Open your ears—hear His voice. Open your heart—feel His love. Let your spirit fly to know and experience all He is and all you are with Him.

This is who He is. Experience. Knowing.

CHAPTER 19

The Three "P's"

Our journey continues—the journey of discovery, the journey of the soul, the journey to God.

Is my journey of discovery different from yours? Not likely. The details of my life are individual and specific to me, but overall, not much different from yours. So, why do I share what has happened to me? Why do I share my journey? Because, as I said before, I wish for you to know Him as I do. I wish for you to be able to experience in your life what I have in mine. It is the purpose of my life—for you to know Him.

I have told you of my healing. I have told you of my peace and joy. I have told you of our oneness and connectedness. I have told you of our love. I wish to tell you more.

I wish to tell you of patience, process and purpose. I call these the "P" words and often times I came close to wanting them out of my life. They really were a source of frustration to me many, many times. I know the value of them now, but the knowing of them was not the easiest thing I ever learned in my life. They did demand work and I share them with you so hopefully, you will not struggle as I did. It is my heartfelt wish that you do not.

Patience. This has been a thorn in my side all my life! I often asked God if this was the purpose of my life here—to learn patience, because I seemed to be so lacking in it. Is this one of those details of my life which mimic yours? Is this something you too struggle with? I believe it is part of the human condition. We all seem to have a fixation on "now" which is, of course, the opposite of patience. I'm afraid though it is necessary to learn it to be successful on our life's journey.

I define patience as the ability to wait for one's

desires without complaint. Does this sound like you? Bless you if it does! It certainly wasn't me. But I have learned this lesson and patience has been incorporated in my life. I can't say I do not long for the immediacy of things, but I am content now to wait if it is to be.

I fought it. I wanted my timetable to be "the" timetable for my life. I desired "now" with no changes allowed. But I learned. I learned "now" was not always in my best interest. I learned with my limited knowledge of the big picture, the puzzle pieces didn't always fit into "now". I learned waiting is many, many times the absolute very best occurrence, for it brings the abundance.

So, how can I help you? What words can I say to aid you in your learning and finding contentment? I can say, "Don't fight it, go with the flow". I can say, "Relax, all is well". I can say, "Give it to God and He will handle it". All of this is true, but I know it is much easier said than done. So, once again, how do I help you? Let's try something.

Pretend you are stuck in a traffic jam. You are unable to move in any direction or take a different route—you are really stuck. What do you do? Of course, you can fret and become anxious and upset. You can become angry and violent. You can become frustrated. However, you can also be patient. You can wait it out knowing at some point you will move toward your destination. The difference in experiencing all the negative emotion to the positive emotion is one thing—understanding of what it is you have control over and what you don't.

You can pound on the dashboard, you can scream and swear, you can rant and rave and holler at the jerks that caused the mess and when you are all done, you have not moved one single inch! What advantage did all that energy and behavior bring about? It probably raised your blood pressure, created undo stress to your body and caused emotional harm. Did it solve anything? Absolutely not. Acceptance of the situation and your inability to change it is what leads to patience. It brings harmony to the situation and therefore, to your life.

By looking at each situation you face, all the events and occurrences of your day and life, you can make the determination how to react to it. The key is in understanding what you can change about the situation and what you cannot. It comes down to making a choice, the choice to change what you can and letting go of the remainder; a choice to control what you can and giving over what you cannot. It is by trying to control the whole situation, even that which we cannot, which causes us frustration. It is by this constant fight that we do harm to ourselves—our bodies, our emotions, and our mental health.

Acceptance of that which we cannot change brings patience. Acceptance however, does not mean complacency or lack of responsibility. We still must change what we can to improve a situation or our life, to bring us peace and harmony. Acceptance means understanding there are life forces that may alter our plan, our desire or preferred outcome. It is understanding that we do not have the complete picture for the interconnection with all of life. It is this understanding which allows us the patience for all those pieces to be "fit" together. Since we are not the master "puzzle-maker", it is best to give up the fight and know we are taken care of.

Learning patience is necessary if we wish to be successful in our life because all is not given or achieved at one time. Each stage of our life brings with it many blessings and gifts along with the newness of the stage. The newness of each stage is gradual and involves change and growth and change and growth is a process.

Which brings the next "P" word—process—again,

one not always easy to accept and another one that I have struggled with in the past.

Process is a method which allows us the time to acclimate ourselves to what is happening in our life. The significance of, the demands of, the changes of, and the decisions of our life cannot be handled in one fell swoop. We do not have the capability to adjust that quickly. We are not equipped to adapt to all of life at one time. So, we must process. We must allow the ebb and flow to run through our life. We must allow ourselves this freedom. We must allow ourselves the strength it brings. We must allow ourselves the help it brings.

Is it a peaceful transition? Not always. Is it free of frustration and upset? Not always. Is it free of challenge? Not always. Does it demand persistence? Yes. Does it ask of us hard work and introspection? Yes. Does it ask us to give our energy to it? Yes. Does it require patience? Absolutely.

Remember, process is about time. Process is about growth. Process is about who we are. It is impossible without patience because time, growth and our essence are unlimited experiences. Process and patience go hand in hand, can't have one without the other. Well, I amend that statement. We can have process without patience if we wish a very, very difficult journey. Our impatience will not speed up process. It will not change it. The journey through process remains the same; so we may as well accept and incorporate patience in our life to smooth the road for us.

Process is necessary for our growth. As we search through the situations that occur in our life, as we reach for more knowledge, as we strive for awareness, we do not have access to all answers and all wisdom overnight. Growth demands we give ourselves a break, so to speak, to allow all that can come to us the opportunity to come. Growth demands we allow it the chance to make us the best we can be. We cannot hurry growth. We cannot make it what it is not yet ready to become. We cannot force it. We must be prepared for it and ready to accept the changes and the responsibilities that come with it. This demands process—the allowance of all that is in this universe to enter into us and prepare us for the next leg of our journey, the next turn on our path.

The next "P" word is the defining one for our life—purpose. This is the "biggie". Purpose is why we exist. It is that part deep inside of us for our life. It is the connection to all other life in the universe. It is the expression of our life. Purpose is our gift to God for our creation.

"Why am I here?" "Why do I exist?" "What am I to do?" "What is the reason for my life?" These are questions I am sure you may have asked yourself. How can we find the answers? Remember we spoke earlier of the one overall purpose of life, to learn of love? We also spoke of each of us having a particular path leading us to that learning, our one purpose only we can achieve. It is not without question, and sometimes struggle and hardship, to determine what that one thing is, but it defines who we are. It defines the choices we have and the decisions we make. It defines the outlook we have of our life and that of others. It influences our daily interaction with others. It leads us in relationships and our personal endeavors. It is what makes us who we are.

How can that be if we don't know what "it" is? How can it define who we are if we are unaware of it?

Good questions. Easy answer—we listen. Very simply, we listen. We are not the puzzle maker. We do not have to know how all of it fits together. There is one who will do that for us. All we need do is our part and everything will lead us to it if we are quiet and listen. We will know the purpose of our life; but we must allow it to be given to us. All is as it is to be if we let it. Our part is to be patient to allow the process for the purpose.

This is not only in the grand divine plan for our life, but also in the everyday unfolding of it. If we can step back from all the activity and mindless noise we encounter everyday and seek a quiet space and listen, we can achieve patience for the process for the purpose of each and every occurrence. These occurrences speak to us, the smallest to the largest, to lead us along our path. There is purpose in everything. It is all part of the universal existence and all, all with purpose. "Fate" does not determine. "Randomness" does not determine.

Everything is with reason. Everything is with purpose.

So the three "P's" can play a very important part in our life, that is, if we wish them to make our journey easier. Our path does not take a continuous straight direction with no twists and turns. It is laced with many, many roads we may take along the way and we must make the decisions on which to follow. It can be so much easier if we learn to embrace those things that will help in our knowing the direction we are to take. It is the journey to our destination, our purpose that speaks of who we are. We have been blessed in the giving of patience for the process for the purpose. We have been blessed with the gift of these helpers. We have been blessed through His love.

For this too, is who He is. Patience. Process. Purpose.

CHAPTER 20

The Universe

We know much to help us on our journey, but also much is unclear to us as we travel. We often feel muddled or unsure or question if we understand correctly what it is we are to do. I spoke earlier of the need to listen, to still ourselves and allow our hearts to hear. Is this hard to do? No, not if we continue to place ourselves in His hands and allow His love to pass through us. It is through love that He speaks, from His heart to ours, but also from His universe.

I have spoken "universe" several times through this writing and it may need clarification for you.

Universe is the whole, the complete, the totality of all existence. This totality encompasses all form of life, that which we can physically see and that which we cannot. There are some who may ask, "If we cannot see it, how do we know it is there?" I ask them, must we always have to see with our eyes to validate existence. May we not be able to "see" with our hearts or our very souls? We all have experienced this sensation of seeing with our essence even when we did not recognize it as such.

Have you held a puppy close to you and nuzzled its fur? Have you smelled the richness of the earth after a morning rain? Have you gently caressed the skin of a newborn baby and smelled its softness? Have you felt the pleasure of the sun warming itself on your skin? Have you felt the joy of rain splashing onto you as you stood in its downpour? Have you experienced the sight of dolphins romping in the waves or seals diving for the fun of it? Have you stood on the mountaintop and felt the glory of its magnificence? Have you walked the shoreline and felt the power of the oceans and the seas? Have you seen the splendor of the eagle soaring to the heights of the sky? Have you seen the clouds taking shape or the brilliance of the stars or the trees gently waving in the wind and wonder at their beauty? Have you felt the sting of an icy blast on your face or the wind rustling through your hair? Have you seen the caterpillar transform into a beautiful, fragile butterfly? Have you seen the petals of the rose take shape into a wondrous flower?

Have you also not "felt" the presence of "something" you could not see with your eyes, or hear with your ears or touch with your hands? Have you not had a "feeling" of a loved one even though separated by distance from them? Have you not given a thought to someone only to have him or her call you at that moment? Have you not needed the human touch or compassion or love from someone only to find them close at hand to fulfill your desires?

Did not all of these speak to your soul? Did not all of these make your heart sing? Did you not "see" the life in them with your spirit as well as your senses? This is the universe. This is the life that touches us everyday. This is the life of unity of which we are a part. This is the force that contains a power of its own and it is this power that we unite with ours to make all that is. It is not separate. It does not stand alone, as we do not. All forces must come together, for all forces are energy and all energy is connected. The universe is pure and is as the Creator intended it to be. We know this simply because it is His creation.

The problem we often have is in understanding how to use the power of the universe. How do we incorporate its essence into our life to help us on our journey of love? Again, the answer is simple. We do it by recognizing it as the Creator. He exists in all life and the power of it is the power of Him. In understanding this, we can learn to "listen" to its messages to us. We can "see" what it is saying to us. We can feel its presence in our life and make it our own. How? How is this done?

We rarely stop long enough to even notice all the wonders around us. We are so busy and caught up in the details of our days and the demands of our responsibilities, we forget there is a world out there. We take it so much for granted and do not pay attention and it passes us by. But we do not have to ignore it; for it is in the ignoring we often miss the Creator and what He is trying to tell us.

Stop. Stop the craziness. Stop the running. Stop the frantic pace of our lives. *STOP*. Stop and listen.

May not the joy of the dolphins tell you to let joy into your life? May not the playful antics of the seals tell you to play? May not the transformation of the caterpillar to the butterfly tell you to let the beauty of you be? May not the gentle wind tell you to be gentle with yourself? May not the warmth of the sun tell you to let warmth into your life? May not the flight of the eagle tell you to let your spirit soar? May not the downpour of the rain tell you to cleanse your spirit? May not the smell of the little baby's skin tell you to notice the fragrance of your life? May not the petals of the rose tell you to let your life unfold? May not the clouds and the stars tell you to rise to new heights? May not the sway of the trees tell you to go with the flow of life? May not the waves on the shoreline tell you of the power of who you are? May not the icy blast tell you to melt the constraints of your heart? May not the richness of the earth tell you to notice the richness of your life? May not the softness of the puppy's fur tell you to be gentle? May not the mountaintop speak to you of your ability to stand beyond where you now stand?

It all speaks to you. It all is for you. It is all for the wonder of who you are and who you can be and it is all from its love. Use its message and its love. Use its power to make yours stronger. Unite with it in conscious effort and make it your own. Notice your world and all that it is. Know it as the Creator. Know it as His love. Know it speaks as He speaks.

The totality of all that is will speak to you and allow you to see. The universe will help end your confusion if you listen. You will know and it is in the knowing that we live.

For this is who He is. Totality. Universe.

CHAPTER 21

In the Moment

In the process of our understanding, the process of our knowing, we begin to desire more and more intimacy with the universe and its Creator. It is in the seeking that we find our essence. It is in the intimacy that we know. So then, how do we achieve intimacy with all life forces? How do we make it so much a part of us it is like our own breathing?

Practice. It's the only way. Day after day, hour-to-hour, minute-by-minute, we must practice. It is so easy for us to get discouraged, to feel the weight of events on our shoulders, to allow the external to control the internal. It is only through the active conscious thought of giving ourselves to the now that we can stay centered. It is only in the staying in the moment that we can accomplish our purpose, to achieve our highest self.

How many of us do two or three things at the same time? It is the norm more than the exception, I am afraid. I know I have often purposely made phone calls while preparing dinner or eaten while doing paperwork. I am sure many of you do the same; in fact, I can guarantee you do. We get so pressed by the clock that we forget the activities of the day speak to us. How can we hope to hear if our minds are on ten things at once and our hands are busy with two or three?

Remember the dolphins and the rain and the flowers and the trees? Remember the butterfly and the puppy and the clouds? Remember the baby's skin and the smell of the earth? If these speak to us, doesn't everything else, too? Why not the sound of the voice on the other end of the telephone or the article in the newspaper? Why not the sound of the car horn or the swishing of the bath water or the pizza delivery boy? Why not the salesclerk's tired expression or the taste of the ice cream cone? These too give us messages, but they are lost on us if we cannot relish them. How can we relish if we do not even notice them?

Only by staying in the moment can we hope to notice them. Only by controlling our daily life and all the activity and chaos can we notice them. Only by seeing ourselves as being entitled to live the moment can we notice them. We often see slowing the pace of our life as a luxury rather than a necessity. It is something we give ourselves only after everything else is done, after everything else is accomplished. We have "to do" lists that will never get done. I am not saying we are not to have goals or not to work hard rather, I am saying we must simplify our lives in order to appreciate them.

When was the last time you appreciated your life? In fact, have you even taken any time at all to appreciate it? Are you so centered in the activity that it has become the norm? Do you fall into bed night after night exhausted, often too exhausted to sleep? Do you have trouble setting limits or saying "no" when your boundaries are stretched to capacity? Are you not entitled to the moment? Are you not entitled to experience the little things that give you pleasure, or the big things for that matter? How can you learn appreciation if you continually experience the congestion of your life?

Now the big question—whose fault is it that your

life is congested? This we often don't like to think about, much less admit. We have only one place, however, to lay blame. We are responsible. *NO ONE OTHER THAN US IS RESPONSIBLE.* No One. Yes, we may point to our spouse or boss or children or friends and so on, but again, *NO ONE* is responsible but one's self. It is all a matter of choice. We make the choice that gives us peace and the freedom of that moment.

Oh, sure, you say; is she kidding? The kids scream, the boss makes demands, and the budget is stretched to its limits—right! But no, I am not kidding. It is possible to make the choice that will bring us into every moment and only that moment. My goodness, what is accomplished by allowing ourselves to get stressed by the demands of everyone and everything around us? No wonder we are exhausted by the end of the day. No wonder our bodies experience so much distress and sickness. We are not designed this way.

So how do we stay in the moment? How do we let the activities of our day speak to us? How do we find our purpose in them?

Practice is the key as I said earlier, but what is it we are to practice? It is entitlement. We are entitled to the gift of every moment. This moment, this time in our life, can never be repeated. It is over when it is over and the only thing left is the present moment. We are always in the moment. Always. We are entitled to experience it and it is through the experience that we learn and it is through listening that we know.

We must allow ourselves the right to live each moment as we choose. We must allow ourselves the right the step back, view the situation and decide how we wish to respond. Maybe we can't stop the boss's demands, but it is our choice of how we will respond to them. Maybe if we stop doing something else and take time to soothe the screaming kids, we will have peace and calm in the house. Maybe the honking horns won't bother us if we put on pleasant music rather than the noisy talk show on the radio. Maybe the overdrawn bank balance will be easier to handle if we learn to control our spending habits. Maybe the guy who cut us off in traffic won't irritate us if we accept that some people are just lousy drivers and give thanks that he didn't cause a crash and injury. These are all choices of the moment and we make the decisions. They are our right and our responsibility.

Practice is done by staying centered in who it is we wish to be. If we wish to be stressed and frantic and chaotic, it is our right to choose this state of being. If we wish to be otherwise, we can make this choice also. It is in making the choice that we practice. We all know, with repetition, comes proficiency. Soon we will have no need for practice for it will become our lifestyle and will bring ease and harmony. We will have developed a personal relationship with it.

The more we are able to take note of each and every precious moment and hear its message, the more we know the voices which surround us, in all forms, speak from the voice of the Spirit. We will know He is guiding us to all we are, our essence and our purpose. He gives us every opportunity to hear Him, for He desires us to know all He is. He desires us to be intimate with His universe, His essence. It is only in this intimacy that we can become one with Him in all ways.

He is this. Intimacy.

CHAPTER 22

Simplicity

Simplicity. It really is a beautiful word, don't you think? But how many of us do think about it and its meaning, much less incorporate it in our life? To simplify means to free us of the trappings of the clutter that is in our existence. It means to reduce the noise, obligations, schedules and material focus of our days. It means to set our priorities and goals to those that bring a sense of complete internal satisfaction rather than external approval. It means to allow "self" to be all it can be. In essence, simplicity allows us the opportunity to truly experience all that life is.

This is the era of the new millennium. Our lives are demanding and the world is in turmoil. How do we find simplicity in this picture?

Do you remember when we spoke of free will and all that it allows us? Well, we are back to this point. Free will=choice. The choices we make each and every day come from free will. Total autonomy is ours. We decide how each moment of our life is lived. We determine the outcome of every situation, event, and interaction we encounter and that of our feelings and emotions. Our decisions lead us to chaos or simplicity.

Let's take a look at what we do to ourselves. We have subscriptions to books, magazines and newspapers that pile up for lack of time to read them. We need our calendar consistently with us to know where we are to be from day to day, hour to hour. We enroll our children in so many activities, they are exhausted from them. We eat standing up at the kitchen counter or while we run out the door to another activity. We spend too much time on our careers and let our relationships suffer from lack of attention. We drive frantically from place to place, errand list in hand. We need to communicate to each other through voice mail and e-mail because we are too busy to talk person to person. This list can go on and on.

Why is it 24 hours in a day isn't enough for us? Why is it our "to do" list never seems to get done? Why do we fall exhausted into bed at night regretting we didn't get more done? Obviously, the Creator felt 24 hours was enough, so what's wrong with this picture? I believe it is the inability to look at our life, determine what is important and to live that importance.

It is too easy for us to get caught up in the dictates of what our society and culture defines as success. We look around us and see others and what they do and what they have. We view television and movies and let them into our psyche. We see the supposedly "beautiful people" and gauge our self-image to their image, be it healthy and whole or not. We determine our worth by our financial portfolio, size of house, type of car and manner of dress. Can you truly say you are happy with the accumulation of material goods? Do they touch and nurture some inherent part of you and satisfy the core of who you are? When you look in the mirror and see a tired and haggard person, can you console yourself with your latest acquisition? I doubt it.

Our doctors' offices and hospitals are clogged with people who are unhealthy and whose bodies are crying for attention. Too many of us consume food rich in calories and additives that destroy our organs and vessels. There are those who starve their bodies reaching for a pathetic ideal that can lead to death. The number of those who get little or no physical exercise is staggering. We destroy rather than care for, mend and heal. When your body is suffering, can you find pleasure in it? Does this satisfy your spirit? I doubt it.

Relationships fall apart or never truly get started because we are not investing ourselves in them. We fall into the trap of going through the motions or "playing" at them instead of dedicating ourselves to nurturing and protecting them. We do not find them a priority but, rather, take them for granted. We allow a connection to die. Is this satisfying for the spirit? Does this bring joy to the soul? I doubt it.

We, who are to be teachers for them, give our children examples of unrest, unease and dissatisfaction. They see us allowing the external to control the internal. They see us allowing others to determine the parameters of our life instead of allowing our hearts and souls to set them. How can we expect them to become whole, complete, happy, productive and satisfied adults when we are not?

Simplicity can lead us to satisfaction. By streamlining our life, ridding ourselves of unrealistic and unworthy expectations, we can find a way of life that is fulfilling and worthy of who we are. We need to seriously look at our life, where we are in it and what we are doing. We need to be honest and be willing to be true to ourselves. We need to give up that which is weighing us down—be it the size clothing never to be worn again, a job that is draining our energy or a lifestyle that is smothering us.

Look at the simple things in life. Would a move to a quiet and quaint atmosphere bring peace to you? Would owning your own business, doing what you really enjoy bring you happiness? Would taking a long walk with someone you love bring you joy? Would a nap in the middle of the afternoon refresh your body? Would looking at family photos in front of a roaring fire bring you pleasure and fill your heart? Would the painting of a picture release your creative flow? Would a gentle kiss and an "I love you" touch the core of you and the one you love?

These are simple things, yet so treasured. This is what life is to be. Our moments, our days could be filled with them if we make the choice for them to be. It is up to us. Only we can determine that which speaks to our hearts and souls. Only we know how the pace of our lives are affecting us, the toll it is taking, and the lengths we are willing to compromise ourselves. And only we, from truth, honesty and courage, can change.

We do not have to continue along the frantic and hectic life we lead. It will however, be necessary to make continuous changes if we seek simplicity. Some changes will be quite small and some rather large. But the changes bring about greater connection with the Spirit. Only in the quiet and the beauty of the simple can His voice be heard. Only in the truth of simplicity can the truth of our essence be found. Only in the complete and joyous simplicity of who we are can satisfaction in our spirit reign. And only then, can we reign with the Spirit.

For this is who He is. Simplicity. Satisfaction.

CHAPTER 23

Reality

Do you ever wonder as your life unfolds just what is real and what is not? How do we know what is imagination or suggestion or true knowing? Can we really tell one from another? Where is the line that divides all these experiences? What are the similarities and the differences? This can be confusing at times and often we give up on the pursuit to knowing rather than pursuing to the truth. I wonder if we truly want to know, for if we did, it may present some challenges to our belief system or demand explorative thought to a wider and more intense degree. This can be a frightening or overwhelming prospect.

Have you stood in front of a mirror, maybe at a carnival or circus, which distorts your body image and gives a different perspective of who you are? You were seeing you, but not really you. It can be a strange phenomenon. This also seems to happen to us as we walk through life. Our perspective of ourselves seems to be what we know and are familiar with and then it can abruptly change, leaving us confused. It is not as easy as walking away from the mirror to eliminate our disorientation. We still have to find our center and become balanced, become whole.

We spoke earlier of all life being connected, being one. Unfortunately, this oneness does not mean we are all at the same place at the same time in our thinking, beliefs, practices, experiences and knowing. We hear and see various points of view on many, many topics and life questions. We hear and see about world and personal concerns, problems and challenges which we have to sort through to a workable solution for all, and it seems there are always points of dissension and disagreement in finding that solution. Along the way in all these differences, we are faced with determining just what it is we believe and what it is we hold to be the truth. We have to look deep within ourselves, and focus with candor and humility to find the place where truth and value lie, then it demands living that truth and that value.

An easy prospect? Hardly. Avoidance and denial are very easy to incorporate into our life. It is a much more difficult process to look at ourselves—our upbringing, values, morals, beliefs and lifestyle—and search within. We have some very serious and tough issues that face us at this time in our world—from political and governmental unrest and war, to poverty and hunger, to abortion and euthanasia, to protecting our planet and conservation, to crime and punishment, to . . . the list goes on and on. We must decide where we fit in this world picture.

Much of our decision is dependent on where we are spiritually. Our exploration into spiritual matters leads to self-knowledge, understanding and awareness and aids us in making life choices and decisions on all levels. The exploration leads us to our truth. This too, however, can be a challenging process.

In looking at our world, we find a plethora of religions, sects and belief systems. How can we be so diverse and still be one? How is it possible to find the One, True Creator among all of man's systems? Can we find our truth while remaining united with the whole and yet be a being of free will and individuality? How do we manage all of this? Just what is the truth? How do we find it? How do we sort the real from the unreal, the real from the imagination, the real from the suggestion? How do we keep our perspective?

The only way is to open ourselves to the acceptance that there is a divine force which is guiding us, leading us, protecting us and most of all, loving us. With this acceptance comes the voice that leads us to our truth. This voice may contradict all we have been previously taught. It may lead us to paths that are varied and strange to us. It may take us to those levels and experiences that we have never known before. It will touch a place so deep in the core of us that we will know what is imagination or suggestion and what is truly, truly real. Our perception will no longer be distorted.

Reality. His presence. His essence. We won't question it. We won't wonder or doubt. We will feel it permeate all that we are. It will bring a joy and radiance that will shine forth from us. It will bring peace and harmony to all of our life. It will capture and hold us tight in it's light. We will know it is our life.

Does it matter what "It" is called? Does it matter

what set of doctrine or dogma or practice it is embedded in? Does it matter how we honor and revere it? No, not at all. All that matters is that we open to it, accept it and live it. All that matters is that we love it and all of it's creation. It is pure essence of truth and light. It is the core of who we are. It is the truth of the universe. It is healing and abundance and perfection. It is unity and oneness. It is all we need. It is love. It is reality.

For my purposes in this book, "It" is called God or the Spirit or the Creator. No matter what name used, a giving to Him of your life will free you totally. He will be your reality. You will know Him. You will know you. You will know your truth. You will be real. You will be whole. You will be as He is. He will give you the answers to your questions.

For this is who He is. Reality. Truth.

CHAPTER 24

Commitment

Many of you have probably wondered as you read these pages I have written just how do I know all this? How is it that I have such privileged knowledge of Him? I will try to answer these questions.

Do you remember in our discussion of dimensionality and the power of the spirit to connect with all of life that exists? Well, I have been able to achieve various levels of this connection. This means I have been able to connect in such a way to the Most High Spirit, the

Creator of all life, that I have a personal relationship that gives me direct communication with Him and He with me. Now, you may be skeptical and disbelieving and I can certainly understand how you feel. To even begin to contemplate we can achieve this is wondrous. I too, am still amazed about our ability to communicate in the way we do, but it is very, very real.

How did this occur? I related to you in my story that I gave my life to Him when I cried for His help and felt the power of His love. This plea and giving began my process of higher development that has enabled me to transcend my physical being and connect in a oneness which leaves no separation between us. This enables us to "talk" in much the same way you and I do with each other only it is not through physical speaking and hearing—it is through energy exchange, or thought exchange. The process to get to this point was often frustrating and painful, but also exhilarating and immensely rewarding.

As I was able to reach higher awareness through meditation, healing and giving over all in my life to God, the development of my spirit "became" more and more in His image. Remember, it is His desire for us to be totally one with Him as His creation. This means He desires for each of us to reach His level of perfection and, in His perfection, He is able to transcend all in the universe. If He can do this, so too can we, again, through His generous gift of creation in His image.

Remember though, development is a process. It is not automatic. Higher awareness must be achieved by "earning" it. It is a process of giving to Him our life, using our choice and free will to love and actively work toward spiritual oneness. We will most definitely have challenges and struggles through this process because our humanness often gets in the way of our spirit. This happened to me.

I often let my concreteness and ego thwart His efforts to help me. I decided how things "should" be. I knew I was right. I determined, often before a situation actually began, how it would all work out. The problem was, I didn't know how all the pieces of the situation fit. I didn't have the blueprint of the pattern of the puzzle. I was trying to fit squared-off pieces into a circle. I was taking my life back from Him. I was not leaving it in His hands. So, I struggled. I cried. I was confused. I even asked for Him to leave me alone at times, but thankfully, He never did.

I learned over and over again He is with me always. He has never, nor will He ever, abandon me. Through His love, patience and guidance, He has helped me to return my spirit to Him time and time again. Yes, there were times I was momentarily tempted to retreat from the process, but I never did. The most glorious and wondrous thing kept drawing me back to Him—the power of His love. I had felt this love in every possible way—physically, emotionally, mentally, soulfully and with complete spirit. There was no way I could separate myself from it because I knew if I did, I would no longer be whole. I would have the biggest chunk of life destroyed. I would again experience my pain. I would no longer know peace and happiness. I would no longer feel the joy that fills my life. He is who made all in my life perfect.

It was through this process of connecting with His love, over and over again, and committing myself to purpose for my life that enabled me to finally have the communication that we have today. It is in this purpose, ours together, for which we work. I made the commitment to satisfy, with Him, my soul's purpose. This was my choice for my return to earth. I desired to help Him in teaching others love, which is the only thing He is about. It is only this that matters. In learning, in knowing of love, we know of Him, for He is the essence of love. In my commitment to help Him, He has given me His power, His assistance in this journey. What better way for His assistance than His voice? What better way for Him to help me with my purpose, and therefore His, than His direct contact with me?

The world is a messed up place. We have taken all He has given us and really screwed it up. We have squandered our gifts, our talents and our free will to create a world where love struggles to lift its head. He knows this and is saddened by it. It hurts His heart to see what we have done. It causes Him pain to know we are not hearing His voice. This leads me to why I can.

He desires all to hear Him. He desires all of us to have direct communication with Him. I am speaking of an absolute, pure and complete exchange of energy on any topic, at any time, in any place. I am talking of an exchange where it is often we have the same thought at the same time. He desires this for all of us.

But do we experience this? More than likely, we tune Him out. We let our life demands, our ego, our desires, our negativity, and our concreteness to get in the way of Him. When we do ask for Him, when we do lift our voice to Him, we want a loud, no ifs, ands or buts response and we often dictate to Him what it should be. We are not quiet for the whisper. We are not still enough to hear. We are not patient. We do not love. So, we move on without Him.

Well, I was unable to move on. I had felt His love. I had known His presence. I knew the joy and peace that He brought to my life. I was filled with His wonder. So, I committed. I gave my life to Him over and over again. I listened to the whisper. I stilled myself to hear. I gave Him my love and He gave me His voice.

He was ecstatic that someone was listening. He was so overjoyed, not only that someone was listening, but also following. He was completely satisfied that someone was so committed to Him that their desires were one. But more than anything, He was happy, totally happy, that she was willing to share her knowledge of Him, her awareness of Him, and her love of Him. He knew pure pleasure in her commitment to this end.

He also knew this would not be an easy task, for the world being what it is, humankind being what we have let it become, with the void of true love in our lives, many would scorn the message. Many would turn against her voice as they have His. He knew she would need all the help He could give her. So, He gave her His voice, direct and pure. It is no longer a whisper. It does not need quiet in which to hear it. It is clear and concise. It is loving and complete. She hears it each and every time He speaks. There is no doubt it is His voice. There is no doubt it comes because of His love for her.

I am this person. I hear. I listen. I talk to Him in the same way. He hears. He listens. He answers—always—He answers. He tells me of Him. He tells me who He is. He tells me of His feelings, His desires, His pains, and His sorrows. He tells me of His power, His gifts, and His universe. He tells me of His need to be one with us. He tells me of His need for us to know the total essence of who He is. He tells me of His need to know our essence. He tells me of His need for us to heal, to forgive, to commit, to give Him our lives. He tells me of energy, unity, oneness and purpose. He tells me of truth and perfection. He tells me of giving, receiving and abundance. He tells me of joy, peace, contentment, happiness, laughter and radiance; and, He tells me of love—sweet, glorious, wondrous, total love.

Now I have told you. It is His voice on these pages. I am but the instrument for His voice. I am but the messenger for His voice. It is His voice.

I do not have to "prove" this. I do not have to "show" you. I need only to tell you what I know. I do know for He has told me. This is all that is necessary.

He is my Creator. He is my life. I know His healing. I know His abundance. I know His love.

This is all that matters.

For this is who He is.

Epilogue

My journey continues. I travel my road to purpose. I travel my road to His purpose. I will share with you what He tells me. I will lead you to Him if you let me.

I long for you to know Him as I know Him. I long for your spirit to fly with Him in oneness, unity and perfection. I long for you to feel Him as I do. I long for you to hear Him as I do. I long for you to know His abundance as I do. More than anything, and with all that I am, I long for you to know His love as I do.

May we travel together—you and I. May we travel together—with all who He is.

Come journey with me.